Wealth *On* Purpose

Your Path to Grow, Protect, and Keep Real Wealth

Bryan Ballentine, CFP®, CRPC™

Copyright © 2023 Bryan Ballentine

ISBN: 9798868255014

I dedicate this book first and foremost to the light of the world and the saving hope for all, Jesus Christ. Without the talent I have been loaned from God, I would not be before you today. I am humbled by the opportunity to walk and share this life with which I have been blessed.

I also dedicate this book to my wife, Kathy. Thank you for your love, support, and putting up with my dream to help others. While not always the easiest path, together we helped change the world.

To my kids who did not always get the best of me when I gave too much to my career and helping others. You are simply the best, and I love you to the moon and back. My encouragement to you is to read the first paragraph of this dedication, therein lies the greatest wealth you will ever know.

Table of Contents

Introduction

Sometimes we learn what we want in life by experiencing what we don't want. That is exactly what happened to me. When I was about 16 years old, my family experienced a bankruptcy that meant we had to move out of our house. We were raised in the country, and the house foreclosure forced us to move to the city. Life changed dramatically for me at that point, and although I was old enough to know what was happening, I wasn't old enough to know how to fix it. What I took away from the experience was a belief that I didn't want to live my financial life that way. I wanted to make different choices, to find a different way to make money, and to be prosperous. I wanted to control my own destiny. Although I didn't know it then, I can see now that my thoughts were already leading me to where I am today.

Fortunately, my parents instilled a strong work ethic in me, leading me to work three jobs in college. Because of that, I was able to make a good amount of money at a young age. I wasn't driven to buy things with it; I was driven by the freedom that money gave me. In fact, at 19 years old, I opened a 401(k) to start securing my freedom for later in life.

I was always good with numbers, so in college I took a Financial Services class. One day the professor pulled me aside and told me, "I can tell you have a knack for this. You should consider this as a career."

Although I was good at math, I was skeptical of a career in finance, so I told him, "Nah, I just want to get a job where somebody pays me a salary."

And that's exactly what I did. My first job out of college was in industrial sales in Florence, South Carolina. From the outside, the job looked great. It paid very well, and I only had to work about 35 hours a week. Although I did well in the job, I wasn't happy there. I wasn't sure if it was the job I didn't like or the location, so in an effort to try something different, my wife and I decided to move to Greenville, South Carolina. Greenville is often listed as one of the "Best Places to Live in the US," and we thought it would be a good place to raise our future family. When we moved, I took a job with another company thinking that a change of location and a new position could make things better. I wanted to stay in industrial sales because my salary and bonus structure were excellent. Unfortunately, the company was owned by a Japanese company, and at that time, the Japanese economy went through some economic woes. So, the company I worked for cut all bonuses, even in the US where we were doing well. That's when I sat down and really thought through what I wanted to do with my life. You see, if money is your only motivator and you remove it, then you are left to decide what matters the most. I thank God that He brought me this challenge to allow me to focus on what was important.

It was not an easy decision. My wife and I had plans and goals we wanted to meet, and the money was helping us do that. But I didn't enjoy the work, and I wasn't getting paid what I had been expecting after the bonuses were cut. All of that led me to the decision to follow my passion and start a career in financial services. We didn't have any kids yet, but we had learned to live frugally, and I knew it was now or never. Although I understood it was going to be hard, I am not sure I knew how hard.

My first opportunity was with American Express Financial Advisors (which is now Ameriprise). Once I passed my securities licensing exams, I left my high-paying job in industrial sales to take a job that paid significantly less and meant that I worked about three times more. It was extremely challenging. Our family lifestyle changed completely, and we had to lean more on my wife's salary during that time. We cut back on everything in order to live within our means. When I look back now, I wonder how we made it through those first few years. I guess it was because, although it was a substantial shift in my life, I knew right away that I was in a better place. When I was working in industrial sales, I didn't want to get out of bed, but now I couldn't wait to go to work and help people with their finances. I loved using my God-given gifts of being good with numbers and with people to make a difference, and I immediately recognized that I had found my purpose.

Our purpose guides our choices which, in turn, provide free-doms that will impact current and future generations. If we can define our purpose, then we can choose our destiny. After a number of years with large institutional financial firms, that is the philosophy that led me to open Ballentine Capital Advisors in 2006, and it's still the guiding vision of our firm today.

When I started my business, my goal was to give unbiased, independent, customer-focused financial advice. I wanted to help clients make smart decisions about financial and investment planning so that they could build a stable and secure financial future for themselves and their families. I wanted to make sure that my clients didn't have to worry about their money. Keeping this in mind, I did what I needed to do to make sure my clients got the best advice and help so they could get the most out of their money.

As a trusted advisor, I've been very lucky to be a part of my clients' journeys to financial independence and to see them reach their goals. I have coached and walked beside them as they worked to pay off debts, build wealth, send their kids to college, and plan for retirement with confidence. One of the best parts of my job is seeing people get better at managing their money and achieving their financial goals. I'm honored they have put their faith in me and have given me the chance to be a part of their journey.

One aspect of financial planning that I enjoy is that it uti-lizes so many different skills. It is a combination of psychology, coaching, being a friend, and being very knowledgeable about money matters. Every day, I get to use my skills and knowledge to help clients make smart financial decisions, and I get to encourage and support them as they work toward their goals.

I try to make things that can sometimes seem hard to understand clear and easy to grasp. Even very smart and successful people desperately need this. I think that anyone can be financially successful and live the life they've always dreamed of with the right help and direction. I know if a client's family partners with our firm, we can affect their families' lives for generations to come. I am not talking about changing the direction of the family tree. I am talking about planting a whole new orchard and bearing the largest fruit for generations to come. That still gives me chills.

You see, if a doctor saves a life, he or she saves one life, and that person will still eventually die. If a family is coachable, Wealth on Purpose can impact the entire orchard of their family tree for generations or millennia to come. Very few professions can have that profound effect. I am honored, humbled, and proud to help my clients live their lives to the fullest and to grow their orchards!

In the pages that follow, you are going to learn more about our company and our process of helping you get more out of your money. You will learn strategies that we use every day to help people grow and keep wealth, save for college or retirement, or make significant impacts in their communities. You will soon see that all of it starts with finding *your* purpose. If you don't know where you're heading and have no clear direction, then your GPS could take you anywhere.

Without purpose and direction, we as humans can get lost and struggle with creating and growing wealth. I want to help you define and develop your own path. I want to help you move from success to significance.

I'm looking forward to helping you build, grow, and keep Wealth…on Purpose!

Chapter 1

Rule Your Lizard Brain

Everything I share with you in this book is going to make sense. You are going to read it, nod your head in agreement, and know that what I'm sharing is achievable and sensible. You are even going to think about how important it is to do what I'm suggesting in order to live the life you want to live. But even though you are likely to agree with what I am sharing, you still might not do it. That's because there is one major obstacle that can prevent you from being successful on your financial journey. I like to call it the *"Lizard Brain"*

What do I mean by that?

I mean that none of us are as smart as we think we are. We are ruled by our instincts, which don't always lead us to make the smartest choices. You need to understand this concept, because ultimately, what will make or break you in achieving your wealth and investment goals is how much you are ruled by your own lizard brain and what you do to overcome it.

Your ability to control and manage your lizard brain determines how you behave, and I think human behavior is the single most important element of financial success. In fact, behavior matters more than almost all other aspects of wealth and investments. Even though investors are frequently portrayed as rational decision-makers, research shows that they frequently make irrational investment choices.[1] In fact, smart and successful people struggle with this greatly and often are unable to see it due to their success in other parts of their lives.

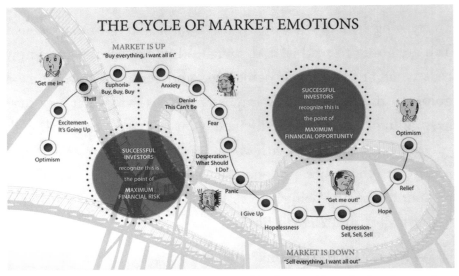

Source: https://christianfinancialadvisors.com/blogs/business/the-cycle-of-market-emotions/

We are not as rational or intelligent as we believe ourselves to be. Our instincts and subconscious often override logical thinking, leading us to make poor choices that go against our best interests. This is the "lizard brain" - the most primitive part of our brain that is concerned only with immediate survival and gratification.

---

1   https://www.businesswire.com/news/home/20230330005218/en/Investors-Panic-in-2022-and-Lose-More-than-Indices-Suggest

Overcoming the impulses of the lizard brain is critical for achieving long-term goals like building wealth through smart investments. No matter how skilled or knowledgeable we are, we will sabotage our own efforts if we cannot control our destructive instincts and knee-jerk reactions. Self-discipline and self-awareness are essential.

Many investors think they make calm, calculated financial decisions, but in reality, human behavior and psychology heavily influence their choices. Even highly intelligent people struggle to override their lizard brains. The ability to recognize our irrational tendencies, and have the willpower to resist them, is more important to investment success than raw intelligence or expertise.

Controlling the lizard brain is the key determinant of positive financial behaviors like saving regularly, avoiding unnecessary risks, delaying gratification, and sticking to a long-term plan. Mastering our instincts leads to wiser decisions and greater wealth over time. Our reptilian brains drive our behaviors, and behavior is the most crucial factor in investment success.[2]

The question is…why?

Let's look at some of the reasons:

_____

2   Dalbar recent numbers here: https://www.businesswire.com/news/home/20230330005218/en/Investors-Panic-in-2022-and-Lose-More-than-Indices-Suggest

1. Overconfidence

According to experts, a combination of psychological and emotional factors contributes to investor irrationality. One factor that can cause someone to overestimate their chances of success is overconfidence. At its core, overconfidence is the tendency to overestimate our abilities and knowledge. This can manifest in many ways. For example, an investor may be overly confident in his ability to pick "winning" stocks, or he may overestimate the amount of risk he can take on without incurring losses.

Overconfidence can lead to an overestimation of your understanding of the market. It is not uncommon for an investor to believe he has an edge over other investors, when in reality, he may not fully understand the risks or market forces associated with the investments he is making. When an investor is overly confident in his abilities and knowledge, it can lead to poor decision-making. This can result in losses that could have been avoided if the investor had taken a more measured and guided approach.

Overconfidence can also lead to excessive trading as the investor fails to recognize the cost of trading and taxes on his investments. This can also lead to losses that could have been avoided if the investor had taken a more disciplined and advised approach.

Finally, overconfidence can lead to an overestimation of your own risk tolerance. This can result in the investor taking on more risk that results in potential massive losses, now or in the future. This happened with one of my clients. We'll call him John Doe.

I had known John and his wife for a while, and they were financially successful. They had a very large net worth. They were invested in real estate and made some good decisions, but along the way, they also made some poor ones. Those poor decisions consisted of chasing a dollar for something tangible. Because they'd been in real estate, they liked things they could physically see. Unfortunately, this caused them to start speculating in things that were obscure, but they thought were insightful. They invested in something that they thought was agriculture, but which turned out to be a farm growing illegal substances. Of course, it caused a lot of unexpected problems, including the fact that they lost a significant amount of money.

John and his wife had made a lot of good decisions and a lot of money in real estate. But then they became overconfident, and their lizard brain took over, leading them to believe things that weren't as they appeared to be. The moral of the story is: If it sounds too good to be true, it probably is. Even if you're a really smart person with many financial successes, you need to be aware that you can become overconfident. This outlook can lead you off course. I find executives, business owners, real estate professionals, and other successful leaders very susceptible to overconfidence. This is where the help of a good coach can be priceless.

Another example of where I have seen people get off course because they are looking for tangible investments are solar panels. I'm not trying to make an environmental statement, but I can tell you, at least in my area, solar panels have historically been bad financial deals. The paybacks typically take anywhere from 10 to 20 years. In that amount of time, the technology could change, and you're most likely going to move. So that kind of investment, although it's tangible, just usually doesn't make sense.

In some cases, I've seen overconfidence in the way people spend their money. They say things like, "I'm going to spend it while I'm young." However, as we get older, what we spend our money on might change, but the amount of money we spend probably won't go down. We never get a call to our office saying, "I'm 75 now, cut the distribution you're sending me." Unfortunately, I've watched people succumb to this kind of thinking and blow through millions of dollars like they were in Congress. I had one client who didn't listen to me when he was 60. Instead, he used his money to buy things like a fifth wheel and tractors. He even spent tens of thousands of dollars converting his gas truck to burn used cooking oil instead of gas. Sadly, he spent all his money on these things and ended up having to go back to work when he was about 68.

> As we get older, what we spend our money on might change, but the amount of money we spend probably won't go down.

So, how do you overcome a case of being overconfident? The first step for investors is to recognize the signs that it's happening. These include an overestimation of one's own abilities and understanding of the market, excessive trading, and taking on more risk than you can handle.

You need to know you are not going to "outsmart" the market, the economy, the institutions, or most any financial situation. We have access to more information than ever. Information is available 24/7 worldwide, but less wisdom is out there than ever before. The truth is, without the help of an objective financial advisor and coach, the chances of an error are very high. This has nothing to do with intellect and everything to do with the *"Lizard Brain"* or *"Human Behavior."*

> We have access to more information than ever. Information is available 24/7 worldwide, but less wisdom is out there than ever before. The truth is, without the help of an objective financial advisor and coach, the chances of an error are very high. This has nothing to do with intellect and everything to do with the **"Lizard Brain"** or **"Human Behavior."**

The next step is to develop a plan of action to avoid overconfidence. This should include setting realistic goals, developing an understanding of the risks associated with investing, and sticking to a consistent investment strategy.

By recognizing the signs of overconfidence, developing a plan of action to avoid it, and staying informed, investors can help ensure that they are making sound decisions and avoid unnecessary bad behavioral decisions.

2. Loss Aversion

Loss Aversion is another powerful psychological phenomenon that taps into our lizard brain. It happens because people feel the pain of losses more than the joy of gains. This phenomenon has been studied extensively in the field of psychology. It is especially true when it comes to investing. Investors are often more concerned with avoiding losses than they are with maximizing gains.

The concept of Loss Aversion can be traced back to the work of Nobel Prize-winning economist Daniel Kahneman and his collaborator Amos Tversky.[3] In their work, they proposed that people tend to be more sensitive to losses than they are to gains, and that this tendency is rooted in our human brain. At its core, Loss Aversion is a result of our need to survive and thrive. We are hardwired as humans to be wary of losses, as losses can often lead to death or other negative outcomes.

Loss Aversion is especially evident in investing. Investors can become overly focused on avoiding losses, leading them to

---

3   https://www.behavioraleconomics.com/resources/mini-encyclopedia-of-be/loss-aversion/

make irrational decisions. For example, an investor may become overly risk-averse and choose to invest in low-yielding, low-risk investments instead of higher-yielding, higher-risk investments. This can also make an investor unable to achieve his goals, not create as much wealth as possible, and lose money due to inflation and taxes. Similarly, investors may also become overly focused on short-term gains, leading them to take on more risk than is prudent in order to try to achieve quick gains.

In addition, Loss Aversion can lead to investors holding onto losing positions for too long, resulting in larger losses than necessary. This is known as the "Disposition Effect," and it is one of the most destructive behavioral biases in investing.

The Disposition Effect describes an investor's tendency to hold on to losing investments too long while being too quick to sell winning investments. There are a few key aspects of the Disposition Effect:

- Loss Aversion - Investors feel the pain of losses much more than the pleasure of equal gains. This makes them reluctant to realize losses.

- Anchoring - Investors anchor to the original purchase price rather than the current value. They are reluctant to sell at a loss compared to the anchor price.

- Regret Avoidance - Investors want to avoid regret if a stock they sell then goes up in value. They'd rather hold losers hoping they'll come back.

– Pride - Investors feel pride and want to hold on to winners, hoping for further gains. They feel regret closing out winners too soon.

– Mental Accounting - Investors treat each investment as its own mental account rather than looking at the whole portfolio. This makes them hesitate to realize small losses.

To avoid these pitfalls, investors need to be aware of Loss Aversion and strive to make rational, unemotional decisions. Investors should understand the concept of Loss Aversion and use it to their advantage by taking a long-term view and focusing on maximizing gains for a given goal and time frame (see Chapter 4) instead of avoiding losses. By taking a more disciplined approach to wealth and investing, investors can avoid Loss Aversion and achieve greater success.

3. Overreacting

Overreacting is another common behavior that can be detrimental to an investor's success. This behavior involves making large and quick decisions in response to certain pieces of news or data, without taking the time to properly analyze and consider the full context of the situation. This can lead to poor decision-making and significant losses in the long term.

A good example of this occurred during the Covid pandemic. I had several folks overreact and try to get out of the market. One of them was a very successful client. He told me that he wanted to get out, and he was going to get back in after corporate earnings had been positive for two consecutive quarters. The problem is that after two consecutive quarters of positive earnings, the market will most likely be ready to drop again. In other words, he was waiting for a dinner bell to tell him when to get in and out. But there's no dinner bell to call you home.

Likewise, I had another client who did something similar during Covid. He got in and out of the market four times (against my advice), and he lost a lot of money doing that. If he had just stayed put, he would have been fine. Instead, he locked in real losses each time he went in and out of the market. His overreacting was costly. One lesson to consider is that, when we are overreacting, it is in our human nature to want to do something. The thing to do is review your goals, plans, and implementation with your advisor rather than overreact.

I'm giving examples of people who wanted to get out because of the Covid pandemic, but before that, it was the '08 crisis. And before that was the '01 crisis. And before that, it was Black Monday in 1987. It could have been the oil crisis before that. It could have been any number of issues. The crisis du jour often sends our lizard brains into panic. But the market is always unpredictable and tempts us to overreact. If it were predictable, we'd avoid the downturns and only be in the good times. The truth is that you have to be in for the long term, and study after study after study show that if you miss just a few of the best days, you miss most of the good performance.

In our lizard brain, there is always a reason to bail out of the market. It is just that, historically, none of those reasons have worked out. Even if an investor guesses the correct time to get out, he has to get back in at the right time as well. I will never forget a client that over the years got in and out of the market four times. He got all of them wrong except one. On the one he got right, he barely got it right. So, all in all, he made really poor decisions. You would think it would be a 50/50 call, but in my experience, it is much, much worse when "smart" people try to "outsmart" the market. Finally, I explained it like this to the client that wanted to overreact by getting out and back in:

Me: "If the stock market earned 10% over a 20-year period, would that be acceptable?"

Client: "Yes."

Me: "Do you plan to be invested for the next 20 years or more?"

Client: "Yes."

Me: "Then what if we invested in the market for 20 years and did not move in or out during the good or bad times?"

Client: "Well, I want to miss the bad times since I don't like going down."

Me: "So, you really want higher than 10% return and with less volatility. If you remove the bad times and only have the good times, the results would be a low volatility portfolio that outperformed all of history. Everyone on the planet would want that. Unfortunately, it does not exist."

We need to be honest about our lizard brain and understand what we are saying. We also need to assess whether our thoughts (either stated or implied) are even on Planet Earth. If most rational people said out loud the above, they might realize it is not a rational thought. Unfortunately, we are consistently controlled by our bad behavioral lizard brain and don't realize what our actions are leading us to. This is where the deep need for a trusted advisor and coach comes in. He can help you see the trees in the forest you are surrounded by and help remove the blinders of your thoughts and actions around your wealth.

Let me give you another way to think about this. Suppose Tiger Woods told his coach, Butch Harmon, "I want to shoot 45 each day on all four days of the Masters each year. I want to just use the good shots and eliminate the bad ones, and I want to do that all four days of the tournament. I'd also like to do it every year I am in the tournament."

Butch would tell Tiger he was crazy!

In my own way, I am politely telling you that you are crazy if you think you will even remotely be able to avoid the bad and capture only the good with investments on any regular, reliable basis. If you don't believe me, ask Warren Buffet or study investment history. If you can agree with me on this point, it will probably save you a lot of money, time, and frustration.

Returns in the market are concentrated in short time periods. The problem is that you don't know which time periods they will happen in. No one is smart enough to know when to get in and out on any particular day, week, or month (that includes you and Warren Buffet). Investor after investor proves this point. In crisis after crisis, the most important thing is to stay in a long-term diversified portfolio. Whether it's the debt ceiling being raised, Covid, the '08 housing crisis, the '01 tech bubble—you name it, in my 25 years in the business, I have seen them all—our lizard brain reacts and throws us off course.

> Returns in the market are concentrated in short time periods. The problem is that you don't know which time periods they will happen in.

To avoid overreacting, investors must be disciplined and take a measured approach to decision-making by carefully gathering and assessing all relevant information before making a decision. Investors should have a coach and not be swayed by their emotions. If guided by a plan and advisor, this challenge can be managed.

4. Herd Mentality Bias

Sometimes overreacting occurs because of the herd mentality. Herd mentality bias leads people to make decisions based on the actions and opinions of the majority. People are often in-fluenced by what other people think, whether those beliefs and behaviors are rational or not.

One area that I've seen a herd mentality at work is when people buy timeshares. They find out their friends are purchas-ing timeshares, and they want to get in on the "deal." Maybe there's a timeshare situation that works, but if there is, it is rare. What I see is that people usually pay too much for the share, make large payments to buy the share (or worse yet, finance it), pay large annual maintenance dues that constantly rise, and then don't use it. Instead, they could often rent something on a short-term basis and have a much better deal. Timeshares just don't usually provide the return on investment that was pitched when bought. Rather, the herd mentality bias has kicked in.

Herd mentality bias can also lead to errors in judgment. People can become so focused on the opinions of the majority that they forget to think for themselves. This can lead to a lack of critical thinking and an inability to make decisions based on facts and evidence. One place I see this happen is when people buy cars. There is a tendency in our culture to want to "keep up with the Joneses." As a result, we often purchase cars we can't af-ford to impress people we don't like. We want the status symbol of driving a BMW or a Mercedes. There is nothing wrong with these cars. They're great vehicles. Unfortunately, most people can't afford them, much less the maintenance, gas, etc. Instead, most people should drive a good, reliable, used car. But because they are influenced by what other people think, they sink too much into their vehicle and watch their retirement future go down the drain or never get funded.

In the 21st century, herd mentality bias has become increasingly prominent due to the rise of social media. Social media platforms enable people to quickly and easily access information about what other people are doing, thinking, and believing. This can lead people to be influenced by the opinions of the majority without thinking for themselves.

For example, people will see a news story about Portuguese debt, the Grecian Sovereign Fund, or some other obscure issue and react to it while having no clue about what it means. In fact, they almost never had a concern about it before being scared by the nightly news. But when the news is on a scare cycle, suddenly we start getting phone calls from investors questioning whether they should be concerned about Peru's oil debt or some country's lithium reserves (or you name the next scary thing). Because it's in the news, investors worry about it. The truth is that you should turn off the TV, go play golf, go fishing, spend time with family, or whatever other activity brings you joy and fulfillment. Not only will you be happier, but you will probably have more wealth from making better decisions.

Herd mentality bias can be dangerous because it can lead to the spread of incorrect information and false beliefs. People are more likely to accept something as true if they see that a lot of other people also believe it. This can lead to the spread of misinformation and can be damaging to individuals and society.

In fact, just recently, the issue was raising the debt ceiling. I had a few clients panicking, thinking that the world might end. The truth is that, if the US government fails, we're doomed anyway. We either all survive, or we all go down. It is a group mission. And in fact, once they raised the debt ceiling, I had a couple of clients not wanting to use Treasury Bills anymore and just invest in CDs. This is an example of the lizard brain working against them, because their instinct tells them to run away from Treasury Bills even though this is not rational. And the reality is that a CD is simply backed up by a bank, which is backed by the FDIC, which has a quasi-government insurance backing. So, if any of these systematically fail, they all fail, and we all go down.

A final example of herd mentality came from a successful business executive I know. After talking to his friends, he said, "As long as Biden's in office, the market is not going anywhere. I want to go all in on Treasury Bills." While listening to friends and/or the media, he bailed out (against my advice). He sold millions of his investments to go with what he deemed "safe." Of course, he made a big mistake. A year later, he would have been up significantly in his original market-based investment plan. He may never live long enough to make up for this behavioral mistake. Now, if he gets back in the market, he missed the run up and is buying from a higher starting point.

And so, herd mentality can be triggered by friends, news, social media, and certainly by politics. It doesn't matter who is in office. I always get political reasons for clients wanting to make changes. "This party's doing this. That party's doing that." And while we may agree or disagree politically at times, politicians don't have as much control as we think. In fact, they have more control of our minds and our lizard brain than they do of the actual economy. The financial aspect of politics and how it affects your actual financial plan are somewhat disconnected. But people have a natural tendency to want to hold onto something—even when it isn't real. That is the lizard brain at work.

> Politicians don't have as much control as we think. In fact, they have more control of our minds and our lizard brain than they do of the actual economy.

The best way to avoid herd mentality bias is to have a trusted coach and be aware of it while thinking for yourself. It is important to remember that just because something is popular or widely accepted doesn't necessarily make it true. Before making any decisions, it's important to take the time to research the topic and to make sure that you are making decisions based on facts and evidence. And when in doubt, lean on your advisor to help guide you to Wealth on Purpose.

I would like to point out another huge, lizard brain mistake I have run into. The mistake is when someone wants to have more than one advisor. The reasons given are usually along the lines of: "I don't want to put all my eggs in one basket," or "I just like doing some of this myself." There might also be an assumption that working with multiple advisors is better because of an illusion that "More is better." Still, it leads to confusion and conflicting methodologies and can hurt the investor in the long run. What it points to is the underlying feeling that the investor doesn't trust the advisor, therefore, he feels he needs more than one. Let's take a look at how this is problematic.

If you have two advisors (or self-manage part of your planning) you have divided responsibilities between two entities who:

- Don't communicate regarding your wealth.
- Don't coordinate your plan.
- Don't coordinate your "buckets" (more about this in Chapter 4).
- Don't coordinate the investment strategy, or worse yet, don't even use the same strategy. (If you believe in a strategy, why would you use a completely different one elsewhere? This is not diversification. It is a failure to have a solid belief system and purpose.)
- Don't coordinate your tax plan. One advisor's recommendation can often totally change the other advisor's

strategy. Again, this means you have no consistent plan. This can affect:

- ○ Qualifications for retirement plan contributions
- ○ Deduction eligibilities
- ○ IRMAA (an extra tax on Medicare part B and D)
- ○ Social Security tax
- ○ Health care costs
- ○ Gifting strategies
- ○ Lifelong tax burden
- ○ Inheritance plan
- ○ Tax minimization strategies

Ultimately, having multiple advisors means you are more likely to make bad behavior decisions, and you might miss tax planning opportunities.

If one of your advisors is an independent advisor and the other is from a big brand company, your big brand advisor is not even in a place to impartially serve your family. In most cases, these brands (and the advisors at these big brands) report to their shareholders, not to you. In addition, they typically don't have access to markets the way an independent advisor does.

You are also very likely to pay more with two advisors as you lose economies of scale in pricing. You will almost assuredly receive poorer communication and service when you add more human beings who need to coordinate, and it creates so many more complications. For example, when there is a conflict with the advice given, whose advice do you take and why?

The good news is that this is completely avoidable. Let me put it to you another way—when you have heart surgery, one doctor is cutting your chest open to fix it. So, if you need a heart surgeon, find one you can trust, because only one person can hold the scalpel that saves your life. In the same manner, I strongly encourage you to find one advisor who serves as the metaphorical "financial surgeon" for you and your family. It's important to have a partner onboard who is willing to tell you the truth about your financial "health." Then trust that he'll know how to take care of it, so you can get on your feet again.

Our lizard brain is susceptible to scoundrels, and they are out there. Bernie Madoff is probably the most classic example. He scammed very wealthy, smart people. I often find that successful people believe there are special deals for them that no one else gets. Madoff preyed on this belief. So, how do you protect yourself? One simple way is to make sure your money is always held with a third-party custodian. What does that mean? That means your advisor and your custodian should not be employed by the same company. If your advisor is working at Merrill Lynch, Morgan Stanley, Edward Jones, Truist Bank, Raymond James or some other "big brand firm," and these same companies hold your assets and send you a statement, you should pause and evaluate. Please understand that the people you work with may be fine people and may even be good advisors. Unfortunately, they work for the same company that holds your money. I call this "the fox watching the chicken coop." I am not making any evaluation of these firms. Rather, I am making an evaluation of their structural setup. Checks and balances are good when it comes to your wealth. This does not mean the Madoff situation could not have happened with a third-party custodian, but imagine if a reputable, large, third-party brokerage firm held the Madoff clients' funds and sent the statements to clients. Madoff would have had one more important check and balance party looking over his shoulder. Instead, he sent statements directly to his clients which helped him to cover up what was happening. The bottom line is that, in most cases, your advisor should not work for the custodian of your assets. And if you have made this mistake, the good news is that it is very fixable.

I've listed a few of the many reasons that our lizard brains can take over, but here's what I want you to remember: Wealth and investment decisions are not driven by how smart you are. Instead, they are influenced mostly by one key thing—*Behavior*. Poor behavior leads to poor results, whether it's investment decisions, spending decisions, the kind of car you drive, or purchasing solar panels. You are human, which means you are prone to any or all of these behaviors. Be aware of this and seek out a financial advisor who can serve as a coach to explain the psychology behind wealth and investing.

> Wealth and investment decisions are not driven by how smart you are. Instead, they are influenced mostly by one key thing—**Behavior**.

Wealth and investing can be an emotional roller coaster, with markets rising and falling depending on a variety of factors. By guiding you through the complex world of wealth, investing, and personal finance, a trusted advisor can help you make decisions that are based on sound financial principles, rather than simply reacting to changing markets and emotions. A trusted advisor can also help you stay focused on the big picture when it comes to investing and personal finance. In other words, he helps you see the forest, not just the trees, and helps guide the lizard brain.

Once you finish this book, I hope you will take my advice. Find an advisor you trust, and let him guide you past your own lizard brain and toward your path to Wealth on Purpose.

Chapter 2

Discover Your Purpose

Now that you have considered your lizard brain and understand the role that your behavior plays in wealth and investing, it's time to talk about your wealth and investment strategy. Since you are holding this book in your hand, I assume that you are interested in increasing and keeping your wealth. Perhaps you're just starting out and want to learn how to invest to make the most of your money. Or maybe you've been investing for a while, but you aren't seeing the progress you'd like to have, or you want to cut your taxes and keep more of your wealth. Either way, I look forward to taking you down the path to Wealth on Purpose.

No matter where you are on your financial path, it is important to know your purpose. If you don't know where you're going, then you could end up anywhere…or nowhere. And you definitely don't want to end up "nowhere" with your finances. Knowing the direction you want to go is crucial to helping you create the financial future that you desire. Whether your purpose is to retire comfortably, support your family, or contribute philanthropically, it is important to be clear on where you're heading.

31

With that in mind, let me share a story that will illustrate how valuable it is to have a purpose. I'll call these clients Joe and Susie Smith. They are in their late 50s and have done very well for themselves as executives in some large, well-known companies. They don't have any children and are able to afford a more than comfortable lifestyle, living all over the world as they travel with their careers.

Prior to reaching out to me, they had been working directly with private wealth and hedge fund managers at large institutions. Joe and Susie were diligent and stayed on top of their investments. Over time, they could see that they weren't getting a lot of value from their investment managers. Naturally, they began to question what was happening with their money. They asked their accountant about it and were told that these managers weren't doing much to maximize their investments.

So, for a little while, their accountant helped them manage their investments, but that didn't work out well either. Ultimately, Joe decided to just do it himself. As time went by, he realized that whether he was working with Goldman Sachs, using his accountant, or doing it himself, the outcomes were all about the same because there was no planning and no direction.

When I called Joe, we hit it off. On the call, he shared his story and told me he was looking for someone to help them create a solid plan.

So, that's what we did. We spent time defining the purpose and outlining a plan for every dollar. We shared our system, our technical expertise, and gave them our top-notch service. Whether they were interested in planning for a retirement that allowed them to spend part of the year at the beach or whether they wanted to make smart investments and receive tax savings on their income, we developed a plan to meet each purpose effectively.

They ended up partnering with us for wealth management and coaching, and I'm proud to say that we have an excellent relationship. In fact, I'd say our team has become their "right-hand man."

Joe and Susie are high income clients, but whether someone is an executive or just starting out, you don't have to build the foundational process any differently. It all starts with knowing your purpose and plan. Think about it—if you are investing without a written plan, there is a strong chance of errors. It's like you took a prescription medication without having a diagnosis or had the surgery without getting an x-ray. If you truly want to be healthy, then it's important to know your "diagnosis" before you get the "prescription." And it's the same with your investments. Your "diagnosis" helps guide your purpose. And once you know what it is, you can create a plan to help you reach your goals.

Here's another example to illustrate my point:

Oftentimes when couples come in, stereotypically, the husband may take care of most of the finances and investments. I understand that not everyone is interested in finances, so when a couple comes in together, I try to keep it as lighthearted and as enjoyable as I can while discussing very important items. It's important to create a relationship with both partners, so we meet with the family to make sure they have a clear plan to help reduce the financial stresses that can come along in life. We strongly advocate for making financial plans ahead of time so that, when either spouse passes away, they have a plan in place that is technically sound and also proactive and empathetically human.

Statistically, we know that it is often the husband who dies first. We also know that when someone passes away, we are one of the first calls the spouse is going to make. When a spouse dies, the widow can be overwhelmed with the shock. We've helped many families settle the financial accounts in their estates and transition to what lies ahead. They've never gone through it, and we want to make that transition as easy and as comfortable as possible. If she's developed a relationship with us prior to his passing, then coming to us is like coming home. She knows who to call. She knows who to talk to, and our team becomes a part of her family. It makes the transition after her husband dies so much smoother. It's like a recipe. The couple cooked this dish before he passed, and the widow now knows the recipe so she can still cook it after he's gone.

> If she's developed a relationship with us prior to his passing, then coming to us is like coming home. She knows who to call. She knows who to talk to, and our team becomes a part of her family.

The moral of this story is if you are a husband (or wife) whose wife (or husband) doesn't want to get involved in your family finances, please love her (him) enough to encourage her (him) to be involved at least once a year. Help her (him) be prepared for what happens when you pass away. In fact, it is something every family should do, no matter what. Think ahead. Plan ahead. Know your purpose and share it with your family members. It is the only way you can continue to take care of them once you're gone.

If you've read through these stories and you can relate to anything I've shared, then I want you to think about this. You need a purpose, a plan, and a team with the technical expertise to implement it. If you do all that in a thoughtful, meaningful way, then your outcome will be much better.

With that in mind, I want to encourage you to think about your own purpose. Take some time to answer these questions, and be sure to include your family in the conversation:

- What is it that you want in your life?

- How do you want to live?

- What kinds of things do you want to prepare for?

- How do you want to take care of your family?

- What legacy do you want to leave?

These are the kinds of questions that will put you on the track of a sound wealth strategy. Review them regularly with your advisor to make sure he knows where you want to go.

Life is short…it's important to live it *on* purpose.

Chapter 3

Create Your Financial Plan

Once you've mapped out your purpose, then it's time to start planning. Financial planning is the foundation of success and working with a good financial advisor is an important step in creating your plan. Financial advisors are often compared to coaches. This is a good comparison since we are helping you work towards goals and dreams and holding you accountable to the process.

Let me give you an example:

The Millers were a young couple when I first began working with them. They were both doctors making really good money, but they didn't know what to do with it, where to put it, or how to grow and protect it. We began by defining their purpose, which included wanting to plan for the start of a family. Then we put a strategy together which allowed them to stay focused. I coached them on the importance of life insurance, disability insurance, and the "what-ifs" of risk management. I asked them to consider what happens if an unfortunate incident occurs or one of them becomes disabled or dies. It wasn't hard for them to understand the risks, because as doctors, they see the risks of death and disability regularly. I explained that even though these issues are not fun to deal with, it's important to meet them head-on so that you can protect yourself, your family, and the nest egg you're trying to build. Eventually, they did have a child, and because they had a plan in place and were willing to put it into action, they did well. In fact, they continue to put money away on a regular basis, and they're well on their way to living the American dream and having many, many choices for themselves and their child in the future.

As you can see from that example, the planning and coaching these clients received helped them navigate challenges and overcome obstacles. It also helped to ensure they remained accountable and that they continued to stay on track towards achieving their goals.

Another story illustrates this point, and it's one that you might relate to. I have a friend who became one of our clients. Until he started working with us, he had been fairly successful, but he didn't have much of a plan. Although he made some money, he just picked random investments and didn't have a focused plan. When he became a client, I helped him and his wife find their focus and kept them accountable to a financial plan. As a result, over the 25-plus years that I've known them, they have accumulated a multimillion-dollar net worth, putting two kids through college with a third on the way. This is where the rubber meets the road. This is where wealth is created on purpose.

This example also illustrates what truly matters. The ultimate determinant of our success is being able to take care of our family, educate our children, create lifelong memories with the trips that we take, and to secure a retirement. All of these happen because we built the foundation with a financial plan.

In addition, I think this story shows the importance of establishing a deep and personal connection with our clients. For a financial advisor to succeed in helping our clients achieve their financial goals, we must build a foundation of trust. This means being transparent, honest, and always acting in the best interests of our clients.

I'd like to share an idea that illustrates the importance of developing this type of relationship with your financial advisor. When you develop that foundation of trust, you can talk openly about some of the most important questions in life. For example, what happens with your money when you pass away?

As Benjamin Franklin once quipped—"Nothing is certain except death and taxes." Death comes to us all, so it becomes imperative to talk to those who will inherit our wealth. More than likely, it will be your children. That is why it is so important to talk to your children now. You need to let them know if the money will be inherited via a trust fund. Also, explain to them the why's, how's, and where's. I have had numerous times when I have helped facilitate a discussion between parents and children about what happens when the parents are gone. This could be when the kids are 16 or when the kids are 50. Younger and often is usually better, but the key is communication and planning. At the end of life, this can be an emergency situation and the help of a trusted advisor to guide you and your family to make this part of life as stress-free as possible is so important. Unfortunately, I have seen when it was not done in a thoughtful manner and the poor outcomes and wasted resources this leaves. Fortunately, I have also been a part of many families' plans to help guide them to carry out this process with great love and care. In these cases, the positive outcomes can be passed on for generations to come.

> As Benjamin Franklin once quipped—"Nothing is certain except death and taxes." Death comes to us all, so it becomes imperative to talk to those who will inherit our wealth. More than likely, it will be your children. That is why it is so important to talk to your children now.

Of course, there are also the questions of your children's spouses. If your child inherits your wealth, what do you want to happen with their spouse? While you know your child loves their spouse, it is also true that half of marriages end in divorce. In many cases, we might recommend that your child consider a prenuptial agreement. These are difficult conversations to have, but they are important to discuss so that you can create a plan that protects your family and allows you to reach your ultimate outcome.

Even with my own children, I've talked with them about what will happen if someday I don't come home. They won't be getting money outright or directly, but rather through a trust. It's not because I don't love them. In fact, it's the opposite. I'm doing it because I love them, and I want to protect them from potential predators and creditors life may throw at them.

A good financial plan takes into account these estate planning issues and builds in protection mechanisms. You're not just dotting the i's and crossing the t's, but rather, you're making sure your loved ones are well cared for both now and for generations to come. The good decisions you make today will determine the future for your children and beyond.

So, how do you develop a financial plan? First, you should find a good financial advisor and coach to help you take this step. Then, you want to consider each of the following:

1. Set your financial goals

The first step in creating a successful financial plan is to establish financially attainable objectives. It is essential to tailor your goals to your specific circumstances, including your age, number of years until retirement, and any other variables that may affect your financial plan. It is also important to periodically review your goals to ensure that they continue to align with your financial objectives and that you can still achieve them. Finally, don't be afraid to adjust your goals as your life circumstances change; doing so can help you stay on track and achieve your financial objectives more quickly.

Establish an Emergency Fund

An emergency fund is an essential component of any financial plan as it allows you to cover unforeseen expenses and protect against financial hardship. Having an emergency fund can also help you save money in the long run by preventing you from incurring expensive late fees and interest charges associated with using credit cards or taking out loans. An emergency fund can provide peace of mind knowing that you have a financial buffer in the case of an unforeseen event. This is a must before proceeding further with planning.

It is advised to set aside at least three to six months of living expenses for this. This fund should not be invested in the stock market, as you may need to access the money quickly. Consider opening a separate savings or money market account from which you can build an emergency fund.

Short-Term Financial Goals

In the context of financial objectives, short-term goals typically refer to objectives that can be attained within a few years. Saving for a down payment on a home, paying off high-interest debt, and saving for a vacation are examples of short-term financial goals. Short-term objectives can help you stay on track and reach your financial goals more quickly. Moreover, setting short-term objectives can help you remain motivated and make progress toward your long-term objectives.

Medium-Term Financial Goals

Financial objectives with a duration of three to five years are considered medium-term objectives. Saving for a child's college education and making home improvements are examples of potential medium-term financial goals. In addition to providing short-term motivation, medium-term financial objectives can help you maintain focus on your long-term objectives. Along with creating a sense of progress, setting intermediate goals can help you stay on track with your financial objectives as they provide a timeline for achieving long-term financial objectives. Medium-term goals can also help you stay organized and focused on the bigger picture.

Long-Term Financial Goals

Long-term financial objectives typically require more than five years to accomplish. These include retirement savings, mortgage payoff, college for young kids, and the elimination of other long-term debts. Long-term objectives can help you maintain focus on your overall financial objectives and motivate you to save for the future. In addition, setting long-term goals can help you remain organized and focused on the big picture by providing a timeline for achieving your long-term financial objectives. Having a long-term financial plan can assist you in determining your current financial standing, establishing attainable goals for the future, and making difficult financial decisions.

All of these objectives can be aligned with a Bucket Strategy (see Chapter 4), which involves dividing your objectives into smaller, more attainable sub-objectives. This strategy enables you to monitor your progress and make any necessary adjustments to ensure you are on track to achieve your long-term objectives. By dividing your objectives into smaller chunks, you can maintain focus on the present and plan for the future. The Bucket Strategy is a key for effective and successful planning and wealth implementation. We have found that clients who utilize a Bucket Strategy have a purpose-based investment income and wealth strategy that can help provide peace of mind as they work towards success. We will discuss the Bucket Strategy in greater detail in the next chapter, and it will be a key take away to implement.

2. Create a budget

A budget is a crucial element of any viable financial plan. This is good for all wealth sizes. This does not have to mean you know where every pack of gum goes. Think of it as getting close as opposed to being exact. However, having a budget will allow you to track your income and expenses and ensure that you are setting aside sufficient funds to achieve your financial goals. It is important to keep in mind that a budget is not a static document, but rather a living document that should be reviewed and updated frequently to reflect any changes in your financial situation. Consider both fixed and variable expenses when creating a budget, such as rent or mortgage payments and food and entertainment. With a budget in place, you will have a comprehensive understanding of your financial situation and be able to make well-informed decisions regarding how to achieve your financial objectives.

The Personal Budget Stress Test

Developing a personal budget enables you to stress-test your financial situation. Having worked with many clients over the years, I have learned that if you aren't saving or investing cash flow you're very likely spending it. This is usually true for large and modest income households. A personal budget enables you to analyze your income, expenses, and savings to determine whether you are on track to meet your financial objectives. By considering all of your expenses, both fixed and variable, it can help you identify potential sources of financial strain. A budget can also help you identify potential savings opportunities, such as reducing certain expenses or discovering additional income sources. By having a thorough understanding of your financial situation, you can make well-informed decisions about how to achieve your financial objectives and reduce financial stress.

3. Outline a retirement plan and strategy

A retirement plan and strategy provides a framework for managing and investing retirement savings while ensuring that those savings will be sufficient for the duration of the retiree's life. A plan and strategy for retirement should include goals such as the monthly amount you will need to save and the types of investments you should make. Include strategies for tax management, estate planning, and other financial considerations. Consider the various Social Security filing strategies and understand how this affects both spouses for life.

If you're fortunate enough to have a traditional pension or cash balance plan carefully review all election options your company offers before making an irrevocable selection. Your advisor should be able to provide guidance regarding the pros and cons of the various strategies. Every plan is different, so there is no one size fits all. However, these elections are almost always irrevocable, so it is critical to take your time and get help. Considerations such as life expectancy, marital status, health, and the benefits being offered by the pension are just a few items to consider. There are also advanced pension strategies, called pension maximization, that may allow you to optimize your choice further.

Planning for your 401(k), 403(b), 457, or other qualified retirement savings plan options is also important. Generally, if you are over 59.5 years old and have retired or left a company, there is little reason to leave your retirement plan at that company. In fact, there are a lot of disadvantages of doing so. There is, however, a special rule if you are between 55-59.5 years old and you separate from service from your employer that may allow you to take distributions directly from your retirement plan without incurring a 10% penalty. After you hit the magical age of 59.5 that special rule is no longer needed. If you are under those ages and plan to retire, there are other strategies that can be used with your advisor to plan for your retirement and potentially avoid the 10% penalty.

Work with your advisor to discuss how the various options may work for your retirement plan. This can be a critical planning decision for many people. With the proper plan and strategy in place, you can be more assured that you will have the means to enjoy a comfortable retirement. More to come on this later.

4. Diversify

Diversification is an essential risk-taking strategy for financial planning and advice. You want to diversify investments across asset classes, in order to maximize the risk-adjusted return of your investment plan. When properly implemented, this strategy can afford investors the opportunity to maximize potential return while minimizing investment risk. Diversification permits investors to safeguard their capital from market volatility, and maximize long-term returns. See Chapter 5 for more details on a proper investment strategy.

5. Secure insurance coverage

Establishing the appropriate insurance policies is crucial for any financial plan, as this can provide financial security and peace of mind in the event of an unanticipated emergency or event. Insurance provides protection against medical expenses, property damage, and other potential losses. Having the right insurance coverage can be an asset in terms of future planning, as it can help protect your family and loved ones from potential financial hardship. Obtaining the appropriate insurance policies can be a great way to ensure your long-term security for you and your family.

Health Insurance and Long-Term Care

Health insurance covers medical expenses, which can be expensive. However, the cost for insurance has risen substantially. While the options are limited, there are a number of factors to consider. Having a plan for this is very important before you retire. As you consider retirement, you may be able to use your company's COBRA for a short-term period, retiree medical, the ACA/Obamacare exchange (with or without tax incentives), or Medicare at age 65+.

Long-term care insurance provides help with assisted living, adult day-care, skilled care, etc. as you age. More and more Americans are spending time with these services. Unfortunately, the insurance cost for this need has skyrocketed. Traditional long-term care (LTC) insurance generally does not offer a guaranteed non-increasing premium and is unaffordable for many. Asset-based LTC insurance can be a good alternative but is usually limited to those with larger assets. Planning with your advisor and family for the what, when, and how in advance is critical when considering your potential LTC needs in retirement. The cost of a mistake here can be especially large and detrimental.

Property and Casualty

Auto insurance protects you from financial loss due to accidents, theft, or vehicle damage. Homeowners and renters' insurance protects your home and belongings from damage or theft. Umbrella liability coverage can help with large claims that your auto and homeowners do not cover. Don't skimp on these insurances. You have worked hard to buy these items, so now protect them and potential liabilities.

Disability and Life Insurance

Disability insurance provides financial protection if you become unable to work due to injury or illness. While often overlooked, this is critical insurance if your income is important to you. In fact, you are more likely to become disabled than to die while in the workforce. I will expand upon this later in the book, but a family disability is one of the additional factors that made me learn more about financial services and wealth management. Think of this insurance like insuring the golden goose laying golden eggs. You, the worker, are a golden goose when producing an income for your family. If you need the income, you probably need to consider insuring it with proper disability income insurance.

Life insurance is also important and provides coverage for unforeseen emergencies. Term life insurance is ideal for most situations, however, there are other types of life insurance that may need to be considered depending on your situation and needs. It is important to consider your individual needs and budget when selecting a life insurance policy to ensure that you are getting the best coverage for your needs and goals.

It is crucial to compare policies, consider the coverage you need, cost, discounts, and potential pre-existing conditions. Reviewing your policy periodically can ensure it still meets your needs. By including these components in your financial plan, you can achieve your financial goals and objectives while remaining financially secure.

Here is a bonus idea on ownership of your policies: When it comes to life, disability, and LTC insurance, it is important that you own and control most if not all these types of insurances. While it may be nice when your employer provides some of this coverage at low or no additional cost there is something you lose, control. You lose control of your future needs. What happens if you change jobs, get laid off, stay at home with a child, retire, or any number of other life changing events. You will still likely want or need some or all of these insurance coverages. If the insurance you had was contingent upon employment with a company and you can no longer qualify, afford, or access coverage after leaving employment, your family could be without proper coverage.

By including all of these essential components in your financial plan, you can feel confident that you are on the right path toward achieving your goals and objectives. Additionally, it is important to keep in mind that setting and periodically reviewing your financial goals will help you stay on track. In the next chapter, we'll look at the planning tool that we use. It's called the Bucket Strategy, and we've found that it's one of the most effective ways for people to maximize their wealth.

Chapter 4

Fix the Leaky Bucket

In recent years, there has been an increased interest in the Bucket Strategy as a way to effectively manage resources. This strategy involves dividing your money into "buckets" and investing each bucket in a different way. Taking the time to plan and invest wisely allows you to potentially maximize your returns and minimize your risk. It also reduces the overall cost of managing resources.

Assuming you have followed the steps and created the financial plan as we discussed in the previous chapter, then you should have enough money to retire. In order to make sure this is the case, we also want to be sure to minimize your risk of having a leaky bucket. A leaky bucket is when investments don't align with the goals and timeline of the bucket at hand.

One of a newly retired person's biggest risks is sequencing of returns. This simply means you don't want to get negative returns from an account you are withdrawing from for living expenses early in retirement. In order to mitigate this risk, we have successfully used the Bucket Strategy. We refer to it as the Grill, the Fridge, and the Freezer. It might sound simple, but we store food this way, and I submit that it also works with money. Most investors and advisors just throw all their investments on the Grill or put them all in the Freezer. That leads to frustration with the taste of the meal, which makes sense if the food was not cooked or stored properly. The same can be said of wealth.

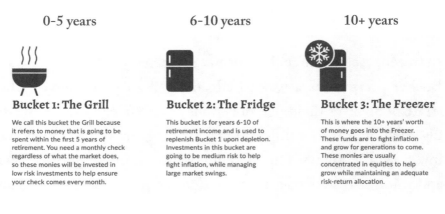

0-5 years	6-10 years	10+ years
Bucket 1: The Grill	**Bucket 2: The Fridge**	**Bucket 3: The Freezer**
We call this bucket the Grill because it refers to money that is going to be spent within the first 5 years of retirement. You need a monthly check regardless of what the market does, so these monies will be invested in low risk investments to help ensure your check comes every month.	This bucket is for years 6-10 of retirement income and is used to replenish Bucket 1 upon depletion. Investments in this bucket are going to be medium risk to help fight inflation, while managing large market swings.	This is where the 10+ years' worth of money goes into the Freezer. These funds are to fight inflation and grow for generations to come. These monies are usually concentrated in equities to help grow while maintaining an adequate risk-return allocation.

Our purpose-based investment buckets are laid out like this on purpose and with intention*:

- **Short-term (Bucket 1):** In years 1 to 5, your money is on the Grill. During these initial years, we'll employ a conservative investment and money strategy as you will be spending or using these funds over the first 5 years.

- **Mid-term (Bucket 2):** In years 6 to 10, your money moves to the Fridge. This is when we're going to have moderate money investment strategies. You should not need these funds until the start of year 6, so we have more tools and options to consider to keep up with infla-tion. However, we have to keep an eye on the clock. Year

FIX THE LEAKY BUCKET

6 is when you start to need these funds, and it will come quickly, so moderation and prudence needs to be considered in your strategies.

- **Long-term (Bucket 3):** From year 10 and beyond, your money should be in the Freezer. This is where we keep money for the long term, and we develop a plan around that. This is also where we work to beat inflation and taxes. This is the growth engine of your plan, and that is true whether you are 55 or 85. You should not need these funds for 10 years or more, so we will invest these monies with purpose and keep them aligned with your needs.

It should be noted that tax status, RMD requirements, and other planning needs and requirements will affect the layout and recommendation for the buckets. Failure to do this will result in less than optimal results. Large market upswings may allow for bucket replenishment before the planned timeframe. It is critical to work with a skilled advisor or diligently research how this affects the layout of the buckets. A mistake here could be costly.

Once bucketed, most people forget the next critical step. You need to have a purpose-based intentional mapping of where every dollar is assigned so you can make your money work for you. This mapping should show what, where, when, and how to invest each dollar of each bucket. If you don't do this, by default your investments are doing it for you. You can take control and allocate them properly if mapped purposefully inside of your well-thought-out and planned Bucket Strategy.

This Bucket Strategy can work for someone who's 20 or for someone who's 75. It can work for someone who has $300,000 or $300 million. In fact, even with our wealthiest clients, we use this planning tool, and they love it. Why? Because it fulfills goals in a purposeful manner, and it helps to make sure that you don't have a leaky bucket.

A leaky bucket occurs when you don't have the plan plugged in the appropriate places. In other words, you don't want the food you're going to cook on the grill to be frozen solid because it won't taste right. Likewise, if you're not going to eat something for 10 years, and you just left it on the grill, it's going to be ruined. So, it's imperative that you map out the buckets appropriately.

An example of using this strategy involves a couple I will call Mr. and Mrs. Johnson. They came to us because they wanted to retire. When we looked at their assets, we saw that they had everything in a long-term portfolio. We went through our Bucket Strategy and determined that they could afford to retire now, but I said, "What if you just worked another year and a half? You will be able to contribute to and receive this year of your 401(k) match, and you could get next year, too. That would also mean you'd get a little more Social Security." In other words, let's go ahead and put some stuff on the Grill now. Let's get some stuff cooking so that when you retire a year and a half from now, you're ready to eat. Let's go and prepare the meal, so it will be ready when it's time to eat. And in doing that, we moved some of what they had in long-term investments and put some things into short-term and mid-term buckets. In implementing this strategy, we had put some on the Grill and some in the Fridge so they would be prepared. That stopped their leaks, and this gave them the peace of mind to enter this next phase of their lives while allowing their long-term bucket to fight inflation.

When someone's working, they typically are just filling up the Freezer, and that's great. We want that long-term growth. But at some point, we've got to take something out and let it thaw. We've got to cook it on the Grill, and we've got to store it in the Fridge. That's what we did for the Johnsons. When they were done, they had a sense of fulfillment that they knew no matter what happened over the next year and a half, there was going to be food on the Grill, and they were going to be able to eat. Then after that was done, there would be food in the Fridge that they could put on the Grill as well. And all that came from a purpose-based plan that said, "This is what you need to do, when you need to do it, where you need to do it, and how you need to do it."

> That came from a purpose-based plan that said, "This is what you need to do, when you need to do it, where you need to do it, and how you need to do it." This is one huge area where I see traditional planning fail.

This is one huge area where I see traditional planning fail. On the rare occasion someone has done some type of planning before they see me, at best, they have received a 150-page document from some financial company with a bunch of graphs that are probably wrong because the data is almost always entered incorrectly. The person creating their plan probably used something called Monte Carlo Simulation which is usually fraught with problems and errors. I usually don't think it is worth the paper it is printed on. Most often, the financial advisor that ran the plan never had a method, reason, place, or description of how to implement that plan or when to do it. And remember, this is the best case scenario.

If this is the situation when they come to see me, it is a "rubber meeting the road" moment for the client. A good purpose-based plan with buckets allows me to explain that good planning must be:

1) As accurate as possible
2) Understandable

3) Reliable as a tool

4) Implementable (what, when, where, and how)

5) Trackable

Otherwise, it's just a stack of papers that has a strong chance to mislead you or to simply gather dust on the shelf. A good plan should tell you what you need to do, when to do it, how to do it, where to do it, and help you monitor your progress.

Another way this purpose-based plan works well is when someone has been diagnosed with a life threatening health issue. Health challenges are very emotional, but fortunately our bucket system provides some peace and comfort at these times. One example of this is another couple we work with. He retired from a large company, and his wife worked part-time for a while. Then, he was diagnosed with cancer. Fortunately, we had our Bucket Strategy in place and were able to tell them that money was not the thing they were going to have to worry about. We had enough on the Grill to get them through. We also had enough in the Fridge to get them through after the treatments were done, and the Freezer was still growing. I told them, "Once you beat this cancer, once we get you to the other side of this, you're going to have money, and you will be fine. And if for some reason you don't make it through, there's enough money for your wife that for the rest of her life, she is going to be fine."

Unfortunately, we've had a number of other people with health issues, and we've also seen some amazing miracles which I think are blessings from God. I've seen someone come in with stage four cancer, and we basically prepared for the end. Incredibly, he is still here today. I'll refer to this couple as Mr. and Mrs. Alberts, and this is where you can see that the Bucket Strategy is not a "one size fits all" formula. What I mean is that this couple wanted to be really, really conservative. We said in their planning, "In your short-term and mid-term buckets, we want to make sure that Mrs. Alberts is taken care of, no matter what. We don't want any risk in that. And in your long-term bucket, let's just beat inflation. We don't care as much about growth. We do want to make sure that if Mrs. Alberts lives to 105, she's fine, but let's design this purpose-based plan with those goals in mind."

One other example of the benefits of a bucket approach comes from one of our clients who is pretty analytical. When he came to us, he was just investing his money in one way. He didn't have any clearly defined purpose. Everything was in one big bucket, and he was always trying to analyze the best thing to do. This created a lot of stress because he was looking at his returns all the time. He was also very focused on dividends. Dividends are great, but real final return is what affects the growth of wealth no matter what form the growth comes in. Unfortunately, he didn't have a Grill, and he didn't have a Fridge. So, after spending lots of time with him going through all the appropriate things to consider, he realized that he had a leaky bucket. Putting a plan together with buckets that don't leak and are meant to protect your goals, even in down markets, gave him peace of mind.

One of the best compliments I've ever received was when he said, "I went an entire month without looking at my investments online." This was a guy who used to look at his investments as much as several times a day, so I know this was a significant transformation. I'm just honored to have been a small part of that, and I'm glad to share that the bucket system works. The bucket plan works in real life, with real people, with real families, and with real problems because it helps formulate a plan for Wealth on Purpose.

> The bucket plan works in real life, with real people, with real families, and with real problems because it helps formulate a plan for Wealth on Purpose.

Chapter 5

Follow the Science

Before you begin this chapter, I want to be sure you've read Chapter 1. In fact, I encourage you to go back and consider reading it again if it's not fresh in your mind. It will be a good reminder that your lizard brain is always lurking below the surface, ready to influence your behavior and take you to places you don't want to go. Once you've done that, then you can continue reading here to find out how science has impacted the world of finance and investing, and why that's important for you to know.

On the bottom of most financial statements or fund prospectuses you will see the financial disclosure that states, "Past performance does not guarantee future results." This statement is true because the markets are constantly changing, and the performance of investments in the past does not necessarily indicate how they will perform in the future. Investment returns can vary significantly over time, and past performance should not be used as the sole basis for making investment decisions. As always, it is important to understand the risks associated with any investment and to consider all relevant factors when making investment decisions.

While the past performance or history of a particular individual stock, mutual fund, or professional fund manager cannot really tell us much in regard to how it will perform in the future, the past performance of an asset category can provide us with helpful information regarding its risk and return characteristics. Knowing this type of information or "history" is beneficial when creating a diversified portfolio that targets specific risk return premiums of the market.

Another way in which history is helpful for investors is that it provides insight into the processes, events, and decisions that have shaped the world of finance and investing. By studying financial history, we can observe how various economic and financial events have affected the global economy over time. Understanding financial history can provide us with a better understanding of the current economic and investing environment, allowing us to identify obstacles and realize that we can behave irrationally regarding our investments if we are not careful.

There have definitely been significant and interesting occurrences that have shaped the world of finance and investing. From the Wall Street Crash of 1929 to the Dot-Com Crash in 2001, the Housing Crash in 2008, and the Covid Pandemic, the US markets have been through turbulent times. These events serve as a crucial reminder to investors that, regardless of the time period, it is easy to succumb to exaggerated promises, speculation, and the false belief that "this time is different." While this time the circumstances leading to the crisis of the moment are different, those circumstances are also what makes it a new crisis.

Historically, however, we have always made it through, and the long-term outcomes over time have not been materially different. It only feels different when you are living it. That is not to say we know the future, but rather, if history is our guide, markets have successfully navigated many crises and have gone on to bring about long-term, successful outcomes. If you believe the outcome will be different this time, you are betting against history.

At the same time, the ups and downs of the market provide opportunities for us to learn. Research has led to the development of theories to help us understand the market. For example, in the 1960s, the Nobel Laureate, Eugene Fama, established the Efficient Market Hypothesis.[4] His research demonstrated that markets are efficient and that it is impossible to consistently outperform the market by predicting future prices. He argued that, instead, investors should prioritize portfolio diversification to mitigate risk and maximize returns.

I appreciate Fama's research because I often see people who want to try and "time the market." In other words, they want to predict when the market will go down, so they can purchase securities with an expectation of selling them at a higher price later. You could say they are attempting to "beat the market" by timing it. People who want to beat the market don't necessarily

4   https://www.investopedia.com/terms/s/semistrongform.asp#:~:text=EMH%20states%20that%20at%20 any,of%20MNPI%20on%20market%20prices.

call it this, but here is what they do. They say things like "I think this current government is headed for disaster, so I want to sit it out until the next President is elected." Or they will say, "I'm concerned about the current crisis of the month, and let's sit it out until XYZ happens." Or even better, "I just don't think the market can go up from here, so let's wait for ABC to happen." These are all examples of trying to "time the market" that are not labeled that way. In fact, what they really are is the lizard brain in action.

Don't worry if you struggle with thinking you cannot forecast the markets. Even the so-called "experts" are terrible at it. In fact, an entire industry of what I call "financial porn" has been born, led by channels like CNBC, Fox Business, and more. I'm thinking about shows like "Mad Money" where the host yells, screams, and uses exciting or scary sounds to make investments seem like a carnival. When investments and entertainment cross, it can be called "investainment" or like I said, "financial porn." Either way, they are bad for your wealth and even worse for your lizard brain. These shows only have one goal in mind, and that is to get you to watch until they come back after the next commercial. In fact, on average, the "gurus," per CXO Advisory Group, get their forecast accurate less than half the time.[5] You heard me right—you would be better off flipping a coin. Now, these so-called "gurus" have countless resources and tools that even the multimillion-dollar investor does not have in his home or at work. And if you are counting on a government offi-

---

5   https://www.cxoadvisory.com/gurus/

cial knowing what will happen, think again. The Federal Reserve is notorious for not knowing when, why, how, or where interest rates will move, and they are the ones who make the decisions.

I am pointing all of this out to show just how much the odds are against you in trying to time or outsmart the market. Whether you are in Dallas, Greenville, Chicago, Miami, or wherever you are, you are not going to outsmart, time, or pick the market as a whole. And the chances are, if you did it once, you will not be able to do it again.

To give you an example of how I have seen this play out, I worked with a client I will call Becky. She came in asking me to "time the market." I was very clear, explaining that I don't do that with my own money, and Warren Buffett certainly doesn't recommend it. Still, she asked me to wait until she called to tell me the market was "good" before making her next investment. However, she did agree to invest half of it the way I recommended, which was immediately. For the other half, we waited until she called to tell us to buy.

Four or five months later, the market dipped for a few days. She called and said to go ahead and buy the rest, which we did. The problem was that over that same four- to five-month period that she waited, the stock market went up in price for most of that time. In fact, it was up about 10% net. So, even though she tried to time it and waited to buy it on a down day, she ended up paying more than if she would have just invested it all from the beginning.

History repeats itself, and the scenario I just explained happens over and over again all over the globe. What I've learned is that no one person or team of people are smart enough to outsmart the market. I've probably had about 10 clients throughout my career who have tried it. I've only had one person who got it right, and I would submit that it was just random luck. You would think with all those times, the odds are that you'd get it right more often. But please understand what you are saying when you say you will time the market. You are saying you will place a trade (bet) that is smarter or wiser than the entire market (world). And your knowledge (bet) will work out better than the collective market knowledge of all investors who have similar information as you. When you think of it like that, you can see that you'd have to be pretty egomaniacal to believe you have the skill to do this successfully and reliably. And most people are simply not that self-aggrandizing. Instead, it's just the lizard brain's control of their actions that creates poor investment behavior. The reality is, we are human, and that makes us more likely to get it wrong than right. Besides, if it were that easy, everyone would be doing it.

Other people come to us with a focus on "dividend-paying companies." They'll say, "Well, company XYZ pays a good dividend" or "I'm going to hold it because it pays a good dividend." It's true that we love dividends, but we don't love them for dividends' sake. Instead, we like value-type investing with a focus on your purpose and goals. At the end of the day, all that matters is that your money's green. It doesn't really matter if returns come from interest, capital gains, or dividends. If you make 7%, you make 7%. I have even seen people allow dividends from a specific investment to become almost a holy grail with blinders. Focusing solely on where the return came from and not the total return is a mistake. The good news is that it is fixable.

The problem is that people don't realize that the science of investing has changed, and they fail to do the math. Back in the old school days, we had huge companies like Duke Power or BellSouth. When our parents had those stocks, they held onto them for what was perceived to be reliability and dividends. But times have changed. Now, if you look at how returns are actually captured, it's through asset allocation. In addition, we know that "Factor-based investing" is a strategy to potentially capture market premiums. The science has shown that small cap, value companies, and more profitable companies are market factors that tend to do well over long periods of time. So, we want to make sure your portfolio is structured in a manner to capture those factors, which really brings us to another point.

I've had executives come in who have received $3-, $4- or $5-million dollar payouts from their companies thinking they will be able to outperform the market within their investment selection. They want to pick special investments, stocks, or invest in special real estate deals that they believe are exclusive to them. Although they might get lucky once in a while, as I stated above, they don't have the skill to outsmart the market. None of us do, and it's naïve to think we can. Oftentimes, after clients have tried three or four times, they'll come back and say, "Gee, I made a mistake," or they might admit to being embarrassed.

But there's no embarrassment in it. In fact, Daniel Kahneman and Amos Tversky conducted extensive research on this type of human behavior[6]. They highlighted the limitations of conventional economic models that assume individuals always behave rationally and make optimal decisions. They argued that people frequently make decisions using mental shortcuts, or heuristics, which can lead to cognitive biases and errors in judgment. Their research demonstrated that these biases and heuristics can have significant effects on financial decision-making, such as the tendency to overestimate the likelihood of rare events and the framing effect, which demonstrates that people's decisions are influenced by how information is presented. I've been doing this a long time, and the things I have truly been humbled by are the science, being human, and the lizard brain.

The science of investing is grounded in decades of financial research and empirical data. This includes theories like Modern Portfolio Theory, Efficient Market Hypothesis, and the Capital Asset Pricing Model. These models suggest that the market is generally efficient, and it's extremely difficult to consistently outperform through active trading. This serves as a humbling reminder to investors that their short-term gains may often be due to luck rather than skill.

Recognizing the importance of understanding the science, I'd like to "get our nerd on" briefly. Let's start by diving more deeply into history to explore events that changed the financial world. This might help you view investments differently.

6   https://www.science.org/doi/10.1126/science.185.4157.1124

Sir Isaac Newton and the South Sea Bubble

Sir Isaac Newton is often credited as one of the greatest scientific minds of all time. But what many people don't know is that he was also an astute investor who was involved in one of the most famous financial bubbles of all time—the South Sea Bubble.[7]

In 1711, the South Sea Company was formed in England with the goal of consolidating the national debt and trading in the South Seas. This company created a speculative frenzy in the financial markets, as investors began to purchase stock in the company in hopes of earning large returns. Unfortunately, this bubble eventually burst, and many investors were left with significant losses.

7   https://pubs.aip.org/physicstoday/article/73/7/30/800801/Isaac-Newton-and-the-perils-of-the-financial-South

The South Sea Bubble story is a reminder that even the most brilliant minds can make mistakes when investing, and it's important to be aware of the potential risks before investing.

The Tulip Bubble

The Tulip Bubble of the 1600s is often cited as one of the earliest examples of a financial bubble in modern history. This period was marked by an unprecedented surge in the prices of tulip bulbs in the Netherlands, as speculative investors rushed to purchase the rare and exotic flowers. This bubble eventually burst, leading to significant financial losses for many of the investors involved.

Famous people who lost money during the Tulip Bubble included Dutch painter Jan van Goyen, who sold his house and possessions to purchase tulip bulbs, only to lose much of his fortune when the bubble burst. Dutch poet Joost van den Vondel also lost a significant amount of money after investing in tulip bulbs and selling his life's work to finance his investments.[8]

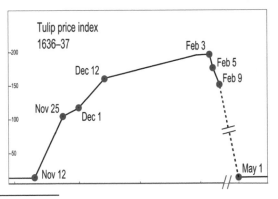

8 https://www.britannica.com/money/topic/Tulip-Mania

The Tulip Bubble serves as a cautionary tale for investors everywhere, showing the potential financial pitfalls of investing in speculative bubbles.

The Wall Street Crash of 1929

Crowd in front of the New York Stock Exchange, October 1929
(Photo: Bettmann/Bettmann/Getty Images)

The Wall Street Crash of 1929, also known as Black Tuesday, was a catastrophic stock market crash that occurred on October 29, 1929, signaling the start of the Great Depression. A complex set of factors created a financial bubble that eventually burst, causing the stock market crash of 1929. In the 1920s, there was excessive speculation and buying on margin. Many investors were borrowing money to invest in the market by purchasing stocks on margin. This resulted in a speculative bubble in which stock prices rose significantly. The stock market crash caused a cascade of bank and business failures. As stock prices began to fall, investors panicked and began selling their shares in large quantities, which exacerbated the decline and exacerbated the crash.[9]

Dot-Com Bubble (1997-2000):

In the late 1990s, the dot-com bubble was a testament to the dangers of hype and irrational exuberance. With the internet's rapid growth, investors threw caution to the wind and funneled money into internet companies, many of which lacked profitability or sustainable business models. When the bubble inevitably burst, many companies collapsed, leaving investors with unprecedented losses.[10]

Global Financial Crisis (2007-2009):

The Global Financial Crisis perhaps needs no further explanation. Triggered by the bursting of the US housing bubble, the subsequent chain reaction caused massive financial institution failures, a severe recession, and a global credit crunch that traumatized the global financial system.[11]

Covid-19 Crash (2020):

The Covid-19 Crash is likely fresh in all of our minds, but it still warrants attention. If nothing else, the pandemic demonstrated

---

9   https://www.federalreservehistory.org/essays/stock-market-crash-of-1929
10   https://www.investopedia.com/terms/d/dotcom-bubble.asp
11   https://www.investopedia.com/articles/economics/09/financial-crisis-review.asp

the influence of global interconnectedness on market volatility. The pandemic's spread caused a substantial downturn in global financial markets due to lockdown measures and economic uncertainty. Though government interventions and central bank actions may have helped stabilize markets, the crash highlighted the value of a diversified portfolio in weathering such black swan events.[12]

Some other events that have shaped our investment history:

In the graph below, you can see other major and minor events that have shaped our investment history:

Markets Have Rewarded Discipline

Growth of a dollar—MSCI World Index (net dividends), 1970–2022

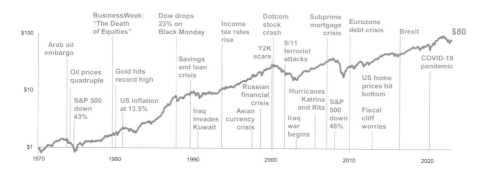

A disciplined investor looks beyond the concerns of today to the long-term growth potential of markets.

---

12 https://www.forbes.com/sites/lizfrazierpeck/2021/02/11/the-coronavirus-crash-of-2020-and-the-investing-lesson-it-taught-us/?sh=79c0300846cf

History provides lessons which allow for scientific advancement, and there have been many advancements in the study of finance. For the sake of brevity and to spare you the gory details, I will summarize just a few so that you better understand just how far we have come and where we are today:

Louis Bachelier and the Random Walk Theory

Louis Bachelier was a French mathematician whose pioneering contributions to the theory of finance are well known. He is credited with developing the "random walk" principle, which has become a cornerstone of contemporary financial theory. This indicates that future stock prices cannot be predicted based on past prices or other data, as they are entirely independent and unpredictable.

Bachelier's contributions paved the way for the creation of modern financial models and the application of statistical methods in finance, and his ideas are still relevant in the field of finance.[13]

Francis Galton and the Wisdom of Crowds

The English polymath Francis Galton made significant contributions to the fields of mathematics, statistics, and genetics. His work on the concept of the "wisdom of crowds" has become an important concept in the field of social science.

---

13 https://sciencetheory.net/random-walk-hypothesis-1900/

Galton introduced the concept of the "wisdom of crowds" for the first time in 1908. He observed that when a large number of individuals are asked to estimate the weight of an ox, the average of their response is typically very close to the actual weight. This phenomenon has been used to explain why large groups are frequently capable of making more accurate decisions than individuals. For instance, it has been used to explain why markets are frequently more efficient than individual investors at setting prices. It has also been used to explain why opinion polls are frequently more accurate than individual experts' predictions.[14]

Harry Markowitz and Modern Portfolio Theory

Harry Markowitz is a Nobel Prize-winning economist who made significant contributions to the field of finance and economics. He is perhaps best known for his groundbreaking work on Modern Portfolio Theory (MPT), which has become an important concept in the field of investing. MPT is a theory of investment that seeks to maximize return while minimizing risk. It is based on the idea that investors should diversify their portfolios in order to manage risk and maximize returns. Markowitz first introduced the concept of MPT in his 1952 paper "Portfolio Selection." In this paper, Markowitz proposed a two-factor model of expected returns, which has become the cornerstone of modern finance and economics.[15]

---

14 https://www.all-about-psychology.com/the-wisdom-of-crowds.html
15 https://onlinelibrary.wiley.com/doi/10.1111/j.1540-6261.1952.tb01525.x

Markowitz's work has had a major impact on the field of finance and economics and has helped to shape our understanding of markets and investing. It has also had a major influence on the strategies used by investors around the world.

Sharpe, Lintner, and Treynor: The Capital Asset Pricing Model

The Capital Asset Pricing Model (CAPM) is a financial model used to calculate the expected return on an investment based on its level of risk. The model was developed by William Sharpe, John Lintner, and Jack Treynor in the 1960s. The model is widely used by investors to determine whether an investment is expected to provide adequate returns given its level of risk. The CAPM is also used as a benchmark to evaluate the performance of investment portfolios and to determine the cost of capital for companies.[16]

The Efficient Market Hypothesis: Nobel Laureate Eugene Fama

As I pointed out earlier in this chapter, the Efficient Market Hypothesis (EMH) is a theory developed in the 1960s by Nobel Prize-winning economist Eugene Fama. According to the EMH, financial markets are efficient, which means that the prices of securities precisely reflect all available information.

---

16 https://www.aeaweb.org/articles?id=10.1257/0895330042162340

Eugene Fama is widely regarded as one of the 20th century's most influential economists. His work on the EMH had a significant impact on the fields of finance and economics, and he is credited with laying the groundwork for contemporary portfolio theory. Economists and finance professionals have widely accepted the EMH, and it has had a significant impact on the strategies employed by investors worldwide. It has been used to explain why markets are frequently more efficient than individual investors at setting prices.[17]

Burton Malkiel's Random Walk Theory

The Random Walk Theory is an influential concept in the field of finance and investing, first introduced in Burton Malkiel's 1973 book, *A Random Walk Down Wall Street*. The theory states that stock prices move randomly and that it is impossible to predict their future direction with any degree of accuracy. This theory was a major departure from the prevailing wisdom at the time, which held that stock prices moved in a predictable pattern.

The Random Walk Theory has been widely accepted by economists and finance professionals, and its impact on the strategies used by investors around the world has been significant. It has been used to explain why markets are often more efficient at setting prices than individual investors, why some stocks outperform others over time, and why some stocks are more volatile

---

17 https://www.econlib.org/library/Enc/bios/Fama.html

than others. It has also been used to develop a wide range of quantitative investment strategies, such as factor investing and smart beta.[18]

Fama and French's 1992 Paper: The Cross Section of Expected Stock Returns

In 1992, Eugene Fama and Kenneth French published "The Cross Section of Expected Stock Returns," a highly influential paper. In this essay, Fama and French proposed a three-factor model of expected stock returns, which has become the foundation of contemporary finance and economics. This three-factor model postulates that the expected stock return is determined by three factors: market risk, size, and value. They argued that these factors explain a substantial portion of the difference in expected returns of stocks.

The three-factor model proposed by Fama and French has had a significant impact on the investment strategies employed by investors worldwide. This model has been used to develop a vast array of investment strategies, including factor investing and smart beta.[19]

Behavior Economics and the Nobel Prize

In the 1960s and 70s, Vernon Smith laid the groundwork for experimental economics. His innovative experiments, observing how people make decisions in controlled environments,

18 https://www.investopedia.com/terms/r/randomwalktheory.asp
19 https://onlinelibrary.wiley.com/doi/full/10.1111/j.1540-6261.1992.tb04398.x

demonstrated that people frequently do not behave as predicted by conventional economic models. His research affirmed that laboratory experiments can inform economic theory and policy, and his contributions have had a significant impact on market design and the study of how markets function. His work became an important foundation for economists as well as other social scientists, including cognitive psychologists who study how intrinsic incentives govern human behavior.[20]

Two cognitive psychologists who incorporated Smith's work in economics were Daniel Kahneman and Amos Tversky, who were described earlier in this chapter. They used Smith's findings to research the psychological biases and heuristics that influence decision-making, and, in 2002, they were awarded the Nobel Prize in economics in the field of behavioral finance.[21]

Kahneman and Smith's research has helped shape the field of behavioral finance. Important practical applications of their research include enhancing financial education and encouraging the creation of financial products and policies that account for the behavioral biases and limitations of individual decision-makers.

These are a few, but certainly not all, of the people who have contributed to the scientific approach of investing.

The reason I share all this nerdy stuff with you is to share the history and just how much scientific work has gone into

20 https://www.econlib.org/library/Enc/bios/SmithV.html
21 https://www.apa.org/monitor/dec02/nobel.html

where we are today. I also want to share that even though we have come this far with science, our lizard brain hasn't come so far. Let me explain what I mean with an example of monkeys throwing darts.

The "monkey throwing darts" concept originated from Burton Malkiel's book, *A Random Walk Down Wall Street*. In the book he asserted that a blindfolded monkey throwing darts at a newspaper's financial pages could select a portfolio that would do as well as one carefully selected by experts.[22] This provocative idea was aimed at the traditional stock picking methods used by professional investors and wealth managers, asserting that their expertise doesn't consistently lead to superior performance compared to random selection.

In a simulation by Research Affiliates, researchers randomly selected 100 portfolios containing 30 stocks each from a 1,000 stock universe and repeated this process every year from 1964 to 2010. The results indicated that, on average, 98 of these 100 monkey portfolios beat the 1,000 stock capitalization-weighted stock universe each year.[23] This result suggested that a random selection of stocks (likened to monkeys throwing darts) could outperform expert stock pickers.

However, the trick behind the outperforming portfolios was not related to monkeys or darts, but to the smaller company stocks and value stocks that outperformed the market over the period. Any portfolio of 30 stocks randomly selected from the

22 https://www.forbes.com/sites/rickferri/2012/12/20/any-monkey-can-beat-the-market/
23 https://www.forbes.com/sites/rickferri/2012/12/20/any-monkey-can-beat-the-market/

list of 1,000 stocks is likely to include mostly smaller companies, and since small companies outperformed big companies, this is how the simulated "monkey portfolio" managed to beat the market.[24]

On the other hand, recent research has found that even the best investors are not always successful at the other critical part of their job — deciding which stocks to sell and when. According to this research, even these titans of finance are no better than a "drunken monkey throwing darts" when it comes to selling decisions.[25]

It is important to remember that these studies involve a high degree of randomness and a specific historical period, which may not necessarily predict future performance.[26]

I share this chapter not to scare anyone, but rather, to show just how far we have come and how much information needs to be considered in a well-thought-out investment plan. Your hunch and your research in picking winners are probably not correct. And this also includes any investors and stockbrokers who are picking stocks or mutual funds with hopes of "beating the market," "timing the market," "sector rotating," "using a rating system," or "special dealing the market." If they get it right once (buying), they have to get it right a second time (selling).

24 https://www.forbes.com/sites/rickferri/2012/12/20/any-monkey-can-beat-the-market/
25 https://www.npr.org/sections/money/2021/08/03/1022840229/why-even-the-most-elite-investors-do-dumb-things-when-investing
26 https://skeptics.stackexchange.com/questions/11226/do-investment-managers-pick-stock-portfolios-better-on-average-than-monkeys-th

And then they must get it right again. One mistake here, or any incorrect decision, can wipe out previous successes.

On a recent vacation, I was near a pool when I overheard a group of Edward Jones stockbrokers boastfully talking about how they believe they could stock pick and market time. As they continued to talk, they eventually admitted their failures to one another. Perhaps it was the adult beverages leading to liquid courage as the story went on. As an observer, it sounded a lot like stories about fishing. After painfully listening to them for about 30 minutes, it was clear they were just salesmen in disguise who had no clue about planning or the science of investing.

One of the world's best known investors, Warren Buffet, said in his 2013 letter to Berkshire shareholders, "Forming macro opinions or listening to the macro or market predictions of others is a waste of time. Indeed, it is dangerous because it may blur your vision of the facts that are truly important. (When I hear TV commentators glibly opine on what the market will do next, I am reminded of Mickey Mantle's scathing comment: 'You don't know how easy this game is until you get into that broadcasting casting booth')." You would be best served to, instead, follow the science, follow the science, follow the science. It changed the world and can lead you to Wealth on Purpose.

So, you may ask then, how do you invest and harness the science behind all this? I would give you this straightforward, but very difficult for the lizard brain to follow, strategy:

Investment Plan Strategy

- Only invest after you have a plan.

- Partner with a qualified, trusted advisor that can guide you.

- Invest each bucket of your assets on purpose.

- Use investments in Bucket 1 (short-term) and 2 (mid-term) that align with your time horizons. Pro-hint: This probably means much of Bucket 1 (short-term) needs to have mostly guaranteed type of investments, and Bucket 2 (mid-term) may need some as well.

- Most, if not all, of Bucket 3 (long-term) should be in equities or assets that have historically beaten inflation and taxes. This is your only hope for real growth. Failure to do this will most likely lead to a failed plan and less wealth. Read Nick Murray's *Simple Wealth, Inevitable Wealth*.

- Don't time the market, pick stocks, play politics, or believe you know more than the collective market.

- When investing in equities, consider these important items:

  - Capitalism is efficient. Don't think you will outsmart it.

- Forecasts and economic bets are usually a waste of time. Most likely, they will hurt you if you listen to them or try to use them.
- Implement a scientific approach.
- Asset allocation historically has determined over 90%+ of return.
  - Be sure to do this correctly and make sure you have access to all needed categories. Most 401(k) plans fail to offer adequate categories or choices.
- Consider using factor-based investments via a properly structured portfolio. Professional guidance will be very helpful here.
  - Use ETFs or mutual funds that have been evaluated to capture factors of return.
- Rebalance with a plan.

- Review the above at least annually, but don't look at it daily or weekly. It will only make you feel an emotion that is worthless (good or bad) and provides no value. Looking at your portfolio more than 2-4 times per year is usually a waste of your time and most likely counter-productive. Less is usually better if your goals have not changed.
- If you want more education on investments, turn off the TV and internet. Instead, read some of the folks

mentioned in the nerd section, or for an easier read consider Nick Murray's *Simple Wealth, Inevitable Wealth*. That book, along with this one you are reading, can provide a great guide on investments and wealth.

You don't have to predict anything, you don't have to time the market, and you don't have to go on a hunch. Instead, go golfing, go fishing, enjoy your family, and enjoy your life. Therein lies great wealth.

Chapter 6

Tame the Tax Beast

Taxes are the biggest expense for most people, and this can hurt your investment return if they are not properly managed. Taxes are unavoidable, but they take a significant chunk out of your income, leaving less to invest. This can lead to lower returns, as the money that could have been invested and had the potential to earn a higher return has been taken away and is gone forever. Overpaying in taxes is a permanent loss of wealth you can generally not get back. Additionally, taxes can be expensive to manage, as people need to pay for the services of tax advisors, accountants, and attorneys who can help them maximize their deductions and minimize their tax liability. In some cases, the cost of these services can exceed the benefit of the tax savings, resulting in a net loss. Therefore, it is important to understand how taxes can affect your investments and to make sure you are taking steps to minimize the tax burden.

CPAs

Before we go deeper into how you can minimize your tax burden, I need to address something important — Certified Public

Accountants (CPAs) or Enrolled Agents (EAs). In my experience, there is a high probability that your CPA or EA is failing you. Although there are some good CPAs out there (we know a few that do a good job), it has been my experience that most of them do the bare minimum. In the best case scenario, they will fill out your forms. In the worst case, they hire an intern to input data, barely review them, and simply push the "Submit" button. Many CPAs have become robot computer submission providers and little more. Sometimes, I've had to explain to CPAs or tax preparers what a capital gains tax is and how it works, which means we can forget discussing a more advanced strategy. Not to mention, even fewer of them provide any real tax planning advice proactively. Finding a good CPA is a challenge because they are rare, but I urge you to find one who is great and will treat you fairly. Making sure you have a good CPA is an important step in taming your tax beast.

The same goes for finding a good financial advisor. You want to be sure you work with someone who is very knowledgeable about taxes and understands the major burden they create when it comes to investing. Taxes can eat away at an investor's profits and reduce the overall return on their investments. Having a CERTIFIED FINANCIAL PLANNER™ professional who understands the different types of taxes that apply to wealth and investments and how to minimize them is critical. This step may save you even more than your CPA in the long run.

Leveraging Your Retirement Assets

One of the things I often hear from people when they retire is, "I just want to pay my house off." Well, that's a noble concept, and may or may not be a good thing. If you want to pay a $200,000 mortgage off using your IRA, you may have to take out $300,000 or more due to taxes on that distribution. There are clearly some problems with that. If you do this, you just paid an extra $100,000 to pay off a $200,000 mortgage, which is a 50% cost of the need, and that went to the government. Consider that against the low-interest mortgage rate you were paying which might have only been 3-5%. Paying off a house or large debt in one year with qualified, taxable dollars (IRA money) often is not the best choice. Oftentimes, the better decision is to pay it off over time. Create a 5-year plan, a 10-year plan, or a 15-year plan so you minimize your tax burden. Meaning, a thoughtful plan that utilizes the tax brackets and spreads the payment over several years most likely will cut your net cost to pay off the mortgage. It is all about the net effect of the payoff, not just the payoff itself. Messing up here can be permanent but completely avoidable with good planning. However, making a wise plan takes a detailed understanding of taxes, investments, wealth planning, and knowing how Medicare and Social Security can be affected.

I don't like most debt, but effectively leveraging assets can be less costly if it's done in a behaviorally appropriate manner (in other words—rein in your lizard brain). The same thing can be said for other large purchases. For assets that don't typically appreciate (cars, boats, toys, RVs, etc.), if you can't pay cash for these items, you most likely can't afford the purchase. This is not a tax tip, but a wealth tip. If you start there, you won't need the tax tip. However, if you make the mistake of skipping the advice of paying cash, make sure to borrow wisely. Meaning, most likely, you should not take out a large IRA distribution to buy the boat.

Social Security and Medicare (IRMAA)

Think your Social Security is tax free? Think again. Think you are going to work an extra job in retirement, and you will pocket the money with no other effect? Think again. Think in retirement you will just take a little more from your IRA and just pay the tax on that distribution? Think again.

What am I talking about? I am talking about the effect that income has on the taxes you pay on Social Security. Social Security is, in fact, not tax free. Yes, you heard me correctly. You paid into it all of these years, and you will most likely pay tax on that same Social Security. However, to add insult to injury, any decision you make regarding your finances while collecting Social Security can change the taxes you pay on it.

As with many areas we have discussed, a thoughtful, purpose-based plan for retirement income should take these Social Security taxes into account and carefully craft strategies to manage this cost. While it may not be completely avoided, oftentimes, it can be minimized. That's because the types of accounts you withdraw money from are not all equal. You may want to use a combination of non-qualified (non-IRA) funds, Roth IRA funds, and Traditional IRA funds to supplement your income. This may allow you to be in a lower tax bracket while also avoiding more tax on Social Security. Let's look at two examples:

A married couple filing jointly in 2023 has the following:

	Example #1	Example #2
Pensions	$12,000	$12,000
Social Security	$30,000	$30,000
Traditional IRA withdrawals	$40,000	$10,000
Roth IRA withdrawals	None	$15,000
Non-qualified withdrawals	None	$15,000
Total gross income	$82,000	$82,000

Taxable amounts on the following sources:

	Example #1	Example #2
Pensions	$12,000	$12,000
Social Security	$25,500[27]	$4,750[28]
Traditional IRA withdrawals	$40,000	$10,000
Roth IRA withdrawals	None	None
Non-qualified withdrawals	None	$4,500[29]
Adjusted Gross income	$77,500	$31,250
Taxable income after standard deduction	$49,800	$3,550
Total tax bill estimate	$5,539[30]	ZERO[30]
Net spendable income	**$76,461**[31]	**$82,000**[31]

27 Assuming up to 85% of SS is taxable income (Actual amount may vary)
28 Assuming only a small portion of SS is subject to tax in this illustration (Actual amount may vary)
29 Assuming 30% capital gains at a 0% rate
30 For illustrative purposes approximate 2023 rate was applied. Actual rates will vary.
31 Net income will vary based on tax bill

While the example above is for illustration and is not meant to make a specific recommendation or tax calculation, it is used to illustrate a strategy that is in the direction of how someone might consider a tax plan in retirement. I realize there are too many variables to cover every situation here, but the concept and strategy is useful to many. Even if part of it applies to you, a well-thought-out retirement income plan should include these considerations.

What should be apparent is that all dollars are not created equal when it comes to net spendable retirement income. In the first example, all money other than the pension and Social Security came from taxable IRAs. This made more of their Social Security taxable. In the second example, the use of Roth withdrawals and non-taxable capital gains allowed less of the Social Security to be taxable. The moral of the story is that the structure of your retirement income is an important component of your wealth plan. Keeping more of what you worked for, minimizing taxes, and growing your wealth are all possible with an effective tax strategy.

IRMAA

As you consider these tax decisions, there is something else retirees need to keep in mind. It's called the Income-Related Monthly Adjustment Amount (IRMAA) Tax. IRMAA is a surcharge that people with income above a certain amount must pay in addition to their Medicare Part B and Part D premiums. It's a critical factor to consider in your retirement planning.

When you're on Medicare, you pay Medicare Part B premiums based on your taxable income two years prior to the current year. So, if you're in 2023, IRMAA will be based on your income in 2021. These IRMAA brackets are adjusted annually for inflation and are divided into multiple progressive tiers. Higher income taxpayers pay a higher surcharge for Medicare Part B and D.

As you purchase large items and take IRA distributions to pay for them, your IRMAA tax for both you and your spouse may go up and up and up, and that amount can be substantial. That's why you must think this through before taking additional monies out of an IRA, because it can be detrimental to you (and usually it surprises people).

One of the most effective ways to keep IRMAA from creeping into the next bracket is by managing your income. This can be achieved through various strategies such as managing the realization of capital gains, using Roth IRA conversions strategically, and considering the tax implications of withdrawals from tax-deferred accounts.

Remember, the goal isn't just to reduce your income for the sake of avoiding IRMAA. It's about creating a comprehensive financial strategy that considers all aspects of your financial life, including taxes, retirement income, and healthcare costs.

It's important to be aware of this and to work with a financial advisor who understands this strategy very well and can help you work these brackets as well as advise how the choices you make will affect your IRMAA.

RMDs

Another thing that you must be aware of are your Required Minimum Distributions (RMDs). Currently, when you turn 73 (moving to 75 in 2033), you're going to have to take out RMDs from your Traditional IRAs. You should do this wisely. Before turning 73 (75), you might want to consider doing Roth conversions and paying some of the tax now to prepare for the loss of control RMDs may bring.

When I suggest this, sometimes people look at me like a deer in the headlights because they don't understand why they would want to pay taxes now when they could wait and pay them later. My response is that you may be able to tame the future tax beast if you convert some of your IRA to a Roth IRA and live off non-qualified dollars until you're required to take your RMD. In fact, this is one place where I've seen CPAs fall short. All too often, CPAs are just looking at today. In comparison, you should want to maximize your lifetime wealth. That means we want to make sure you pay as little tax over the rest of your life, not just today. This lets you grow and keep more of your wealth for life.

I love Roth IRAs. I think they're one of the greatest tax tools out there for the long term. However, when high-income folks are near their retirement, the better solution is often to use a

TAME THE TAX BEAST

deductible IRA or a deductible 401(k) and convert the funds to a Roth IRA later on when retired.

It's also possible you fall into a problem that I hear from a lot of people in 401(k) plans, even very wealthy, high-income earners (HIE). They'll say, "I've been doing a Roth 401(k)."

I ask, "Why are you doing that?"

The high-income earner responds, "Well, the 401(k) guy came in at work and told me I should do that."

My mistake-sensing radar goes up as I then ask, "Oh, really? Well, how long have you known this 401(k) guy?" and "What are this 401(k) guy's qualifications?" and "What did he do to analyze this recommendation for you?"

The high-income earner may say—"I just met him last week. He was the new 26-year-old representative for XYZ firm." Typically, they start to see the light at this point as they begin to realize what I'm getting at.

Think about it. Your "401(k) guy" probably has very little experience and most likely isn't a CFP® professional. He doesn't know you, and he doesn't know your plan. Instead, you need to develop a plan to tame the tax beast. It is critical that all workers, and especially those in their highest earning years (typically 50-65) and HIE employees, understand that not all 401(k) contribution types are equally efficient. The choice here could cost you or save you a huge tax bill for years to come. You need to know where the taxes are coming from—the left, the right, the under, the over, the now, and the later. I will say again that I love Roth IRAs. They are one of my favorite tools, but I see them misused and misappropriated all the time, especially by end users and 401(k) representatives. If you don't evaluate all angles, you will most likely pay more in tax for the rest of your life.

Before I move on from the 401(k), there is one more thing I'd like to point out. Your retirement account is not a cookie jar. Oftentimes, I see people who worked for a company that took good care of them and gave them big benefits, or maybe they worked to earn a pension in retirement. Now, all of a sudden, they have access to a half-million dollar pension and their 401(k), which is maybe another million, and they start just taking it. You're going to pay a lot in taxes if you do that. You need the right purpose-based, bucketed plan. Knowing what to pay and how to mitigate the tax impact is critical. We see so many errors with this; I cannot stress this enough. A well-thought-out bucket plan for retirement (see Chapter 4) that considers taxes, alongside your income and investment plan, is key to controlling and limiting taxes, as well as growing your Wealth on Purpose.

Charitable Contributions

Let's move onto a discussion about charitable contributions. If you are someone who is inclined to donate to charitable causes, then you need to know about qualified charitable distributions (QCDs) and donor-advised funds (DAFs), because they are often underutilized.

QCD

If you are over 70 ½ and you're giving to a charity (including your church), you very likely should want to consider using a QCD. This is a strategy where you give money from your IRA directly to a church or another nonprofit organization. It's non-taxable (better than a deduction), which is terrific, and fortunately, most tax preparers are finally waking up to this. However, there are many, many tax preparers who are still filling out the tax returns incorrectly on QCDs. So, be careful about this and make sure that the tax forms are filled out properly.

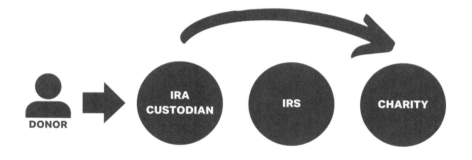

Source: https://www.givedirectly.org/qualified-charitable-distributions/

Here's where I see things go wrong—on the 1099 form the IRS does not have a way to note if something is a QCD. An example would be someone who takes out $30,000 from an IRA and gives half of it directly to a charity from the IRA. The IRA owner receives the rest and spends that other half. So, $15,000 went to charity and $15,000 went to the IRA owner. His tax returns should say he took out $30,000 but only $15,000 was taxable. All too often we see $30,000 is noted as taken out and $30,000 as taxable. That's inaccurate and would cause an over-payment if a QCD was involved. It can be fixed in an amend-ment, but it is still a warning for both tax preparers and for tax-payers to watch for this. Good news—if you are RMD status, a QCD also counts towards your RMD on a tax-free basis. This is a double win.

DAF

The other thing I think is underutilized is something called a donor-advised fund (DAF- a charitable investment account used to support charitable causes). This is where you can give highly appreciated stock or investments, mutual funds, etc., to a DAF. When you do that, if held for one year prior to the gift, you get to claim the full value of the stock or investment the day you gave it as a total gift. For instance, let's say you gave Apple stock, and it was worth $10,000 the day you gave it. You'd get to claim that as a $10,000 gift for that year, and then the DAF could sell Apple at no tax cost because the DAF is a charity in a 0% tax bracket.

Why would you want to consider doing this?

Well, if you wanted to give $10,000 to your church, you could keep the $10,000 cash you planned to give the church and instead, donate the $10,000 in stock. You could then invest the $10,000 that you have in your checking account. All you've done is cut the IRS out. The beauty of this is that you've wiped away your gain, given the stock away, raised your cost basis in reinvesting, let the charity sell it, and the church or the non-profit still gets the money. This is a great strategy to consider if you are charitably inclined. However, most accountants will never recommend this because they're too busy preparing forms and doing audits. Once brought to them, however, they will almost always agree with this strategy, because it is highly effective when used properly.

Gifts to Your Children

This strategy can work well if you have children. You might want to gift your children investment shares instead of cash, especially if they're out of school and, say, in their 30s. That's because you don't have to worry about something called the Kiddie Tax. Let's say you give your kids $10,000 a year for a Christmas gift. Instead, why not give them $10,000 of investments? Let them sell it at their capital gains rate, which is probably lower than yours.

Ultimately, taxes can be a major burden, so understanding how to minimize them can help you maximize your returns and reduce your tax liability. The tax savings alone will probably pay for any fee you pay a good financial planner to develop the plan. Although people often come in to see us because they want to invest, however, it truly is about what you keep which makes this a critical area to consider in wealth management.

One other thought on gifting, be careful of giving too much or not enough to charity and children. I see both happen. I see the parents that give so much that they go broke. I also see the parents that could give, but hold onto every dime until they die at 90, while their children are 66 and retired themselves. Seeing the joy and fulfillment of your children, grandchildren, or charity through a well-thought-out gifting plan can be one of life's greatest joys. You may harm yourself by giving too much, but don't rob yourself of the joy of seeing others succeed in your family or community if you can afford it. While there may not be a perfect formula here because there are many variables, a trusted advisor can help you craft a thoughtful plan that is responsible and meaningful.

By taking advantage of tax-advantaged accounts and deductions, you can effectively tame the tax beast.

Here is a summary of some good tax strategies when it comes to investing and wealth:

- Take advantage of tax-advantaged accounts, such as Individual Retirement Accounts (IRAs) and 401(k) plans, to put money away for retirement and grow investments tax-deferred.
- Use Roth contributions and conversions correctly.

- Make sure to understand the different types of taxes that apply to investments, such as capital gains taxes, dividend taxes, and interest taxes.

- Consider investing in tax-free bonds and other tax-exempt investments (do the math first to see if this is applicable).

- Consider investing in tax-efficient ETFs.

- Do not forget to account for tax on your Social Security.

- Be aware of IRMAA.

- Consider gifting kids and DAFs through appreciated investments rather than cash.

- Use a QCD with your IRA if over 70.5 and you give to charitable causes that qualify. This can count towards your RMD if applicable.

- Structure your retirement income to maximize the wealth you keep.

- Hire a knowledgeable CFP® professional who can make sure you take advantage of any tax strategies that may be available.

Chapter 7

Turbocharge Your Wealth

So, now that you have all of this information, what in the world do you do next?

First, know that whether you are a millionaire many times over or just starting out, you can have, grow, and keep wealth on purpose. It requires effort, but there is a path, and it is achievable. The question is what to do now and how to move from success to significance.

> The question is what to do now and how to move from success to significance.

Up until now, I have not shared one of the other reasons I am passionate about this business and helping people plan for Wealth on Purpose. In the introduction, I shared part of my childhood story and what led me to this career path. The other part of that story is that, during my childhood, my mom's health deteriorated. She had multiple vertebrae fused during a major back surgery when I was a kid. Back then, she had to travel to Minneapolis to get this special surgery. I will never forget seeing her come off the plane with a halo-type medical apparatus screwed to her head. How that affected my mom physically may be something that will never leave me. More importantly, I saw the financial aftereffects of this devastating medical condition. It prevented my mom from working. She was a nurse, so she had the opportunity to be employed and the skill set to do so, but her body failed her through no fault of her own. When she tried to work, it limited how much she could do. This situation, coupled with my dad's failing business, was a deadly combination. It led to poor financial choices and hard financial times for our family.

Unfortunately, my mom and dad never had a financial advisor. The truth is, I doubt they would have listened to one if they did. I mean no disrespect to them. This is just the honest truth for them and for many Americans. If they had a trusted advisor, that person could have coached them and told them to plan for the disability prior to it happening. My mom would have still been disabled, but the financial story might have ended differently. Although my mom had these medical issues, Social Security disability would never approve her for disability in her 30s because of her training and skill set. But if my mom had taken out proper, private disability insurance, she could have received disability income replacement when she couldn't work. Quality private insurance often will pay when Social Security will not. If my dad had a business coach and advisor, he might have been able to weather the storm. The point is, don't depend on Social Security or your government to care for you. Also, seek the the advice of qualified professionals prior to an emergency. My parents did what their parents did. They woke up and lived each day, but they never sought the help of a trusted advisor to guide them through these important decisions.

So why have I spent so much time talking about the need of a trusted advisor and coach when it comes to your wealth? And why bother if you are already successful? I'll tell you why. You see, the most successful and decorated players in the most competitive sports in the world have coaches. Tiger Woods has a coach. Michael Jordan had a coach. These elite of the elite know that to get better and to take their game to where they want to go, they need help. They also know they have to follow their coach's advice; otherwise, what's the point? They know that they have to do the work, meaning they can't just show up and say, "Okay, coach, do it for me." Nor do they say, "Thanks for the advice; now I am all good." Instead, they methodically approach their sport with discipline, coaching, practice, practice, and more practice. Then when they achieve one level, they seek advice on how to breakthrough to the next level and continue to practice, practice, and practice.

Wealth on Purpose is a little bit like that. It's a participatory sport, and it's also a contact sport. Your advisor can show you the way. He can lead you to better choices and opportunities.

He can guide you to things you may have never thought of. He can lead you away from disasters that you can't see. He can help cover your weaknesses and point out blind spots. He can add strategies to your family that can change the economics for generations to come. But he can't do it for you. This is a team sport which I often equate to football. Your financial advisor may be your quarterback. He may be able to pass the ball 50 yards on a dime, but he needs others to help make the touchdowns. Similar to the way a quarterback needs wide receivers, running backs, linemen, tight ends, and a center, a financial advisor needs CPAs, estate planning attorneys, realtors, mortgage brokers, and insurance specialists. More importantly, remember that you are the owner of the team. You have to provide the resources for the quarterback to lead the team to victory. When the quarterback says the team needs a new wide receiver (maybe a CPA, for example), the owner should listen.

I use all of these sports analogies to help people relate and to be very real about the fact that, no matter your level of success with money, a good financial advisor is invaluable. In fact, I believe that without the help of a knowledgeable and caring advisor, very few people will make it to the end of life with the wealth they could have acquired. And even fewer families will pass along their wealth to those they love without the help of this same advisor.

We can review all the technical reasons and debate the how's and why's of wealth, but our lizard brain simply can't see all the obstacles. We, as humans, are not wired to do that objectively for ourselves, no matter what our IQ is or our level of success.

At this point, you should be saying, "I know these elite world class athletes needed a coach to achieve what they did, but I'm all good. I have $5 million or $10 million in the bank, and I can do the math. I've got enough, and I am going to be okay with or without an advisor."

My answer is, "You may be okay. In fact, Tiger Woods would have been *okay* without his coach, Butch Harmon, Jr., but he was *great* with him. He became arguably the best golfer the world has ever known. So, what if your $7 million in the bank could become $15 million by making different decisions? What if you could pay $1 million less in taxes over your lifetime? What if you could pass down all of your wealth to your kids instead of the bureaucracy of the US federal government taking it? What if you could protect your daughter from the financial strain of a divorce, robbing her of her inheritance after you died? What if you simply had more fun and a better quality of life with less worry?"

You see, you don't need to take my word for this. Study after study shows that working with a qualified advisor can add multiples to your wealth. In fact, the ultimate cheapskate in investments, Vanguard, published a study as part of their "Advisor's Alpha" concept which was originally introduced in 2001. It is periodically updated with research papers outlining the value that financial advisors can bring to their clients. The research delves into how advisors can add value, or alpha, through re-lationship-based services such as financial planning, discipline, and guidance, rather than by attempting to outperform the market.[32]

As per the research, investors who work with advisors can gain about 3% per year in value for their investments, compared to what they would get by not employing an advisor. The exact percentage can vary and may be based on factors such as the specific strategies used by the advisor, the investor's individual circumstances, and market conditions.[33]

The study also points out several ways in which advisors add value, including providing suitable investment recommen-dations, regular rebalancing of portfolios, developing spending strategies for retirement income, and offering guidance to help clients adhere to a financial plan.[34]

The premise of the "Advisor's Alpha" concept is that the additional annual gain an individual gets from working with an advisor more than justifies the fee that the advisor charges, which can serve as a marketing point for advisors.[35]

It should be noted that while Vanguard's research suggests that working with a financial advisor can increase investment returns, the actual benefits will depend on a variety of factors, including the quality of the advice provided by the financial

32 https://seekingalpha.com/article/4045415-what-is-value-of-advisor-vanguard-totes-up-advisors-alpha
33 https://ptmwealth.com/articles/vanguard-working-with-an-advisor-can-add-about-3-in-net-returns
34 https://ptmwealth.com/articles/vanguard-working-with-an-advisor-can-add-about-3-in-net-returns
35 https://seekingalpha.com/article/4045415-what-is-value-of-advisor-vanguard-totes-up-advisors-alpha

advisor, the investor's circumstances and behavior, and the performance of financial markets.

But let's say you are stubborn and just "like doing this" on your own. If that's the case, I am not sure what the goal is. If it is less wealth, more taxes, more stress, and no plan for the day when you don't come home, then keep doing what you're doing and don't use a trusted advisor. If this is you, I recommend that you research as much as possible, continually enroll in college classes to learn new strategies that are ever-changing, and live in a cave with computers and spreadsheets knowing that all this work will most likely produce worse outcomes and more misery than was ever required of life. But only do that if you enjoy it and know that I wish you good luck.

For the rest of the world, let's keep going and take some time to talk about how to turbocharge your wealth.

What an advisor cannot do:

- Walk the walk for you.
- Gather the information for you.
- Make all the decisions for you.
- Do it without your participation.
- Time the market or outsmart the markets at all times.
- Want a particular level of success more than you.

What an advisor can do:

- Help you achieve, grow, and keep Wealth on Purpose.

- Serve as a trusted resource to improve the quality of your life and your family's wealth for generations to come.

- Help you lower taxes and reduce this lifelong absorbent cost.

- Provide a purpose-based plan for wealth that includes a bucketed approach to your income needs.

- Help you feel comfortable with your decisions to retire and show you a path to shine in this time of life.

- Guide you beyond your lizard brain and help you manage and direct your behavioral choices that impede you from achieving the wealth you otherwise would have.

- Serve to provide risk management in many areas: investments, property, liability, tax, etc.

- Save you from making mistakes you can't unmake and that are costly (one caught and saved error on your family's behalf may pay for a lifetime of your advisor's cost).

- Guide your family to wealth that is kept for generations to come through thoughtful financial and estate planning.

- Help you impact your community in a more meaningful and efficient way.

- Help move your family from success to significance.

What you cannot or should not do:

- Try to do this alone. Unless you are very exceptionally rare, you will be less successful without help.
- Time the market on a consistent basis with skill.
- Outperform the financial markets on a regular basis with skill.
- Objectively see the forest you are in due to the trees around you.
- Hire more than one primary advisor. (Using more than one advisor is a tremendous and potentially financially fatal error that is completely avoidable. Reread Chapter 1.)
- Have and maintain the ongoing planning and technical training needed to keep up with and have access to all the changing opportunities in the financial investment world (unless you are a very, very rare anomaly).

What you can do:

- Partner with a trusted advisor to develop a purpose-based plan.
- Participate in your process—gather data, return phone calls and emails, go to meetings with your advisor, implement sensible advice.
- Live a life full of purpose.

- Have, Keep, Protect, and Grow Wealth on Purpose.

———◦———

I have shared a lot of stories, outcomes, and solutions in this book. I want to leave you with one more personal story. When my son was born, my wife, Kathy, quit her job outside the home and began the hardest job in the world that you can do without pay. She stayed at home full-time with our son. A little while after he was born, she received the bill for her disability insurance policy. Thankfully, she had a great advisor (me) who had coached her to get a disability insurance policy while she was working prior to our son's birth. When the bill came in, she asked, "Should we cancel this policy since I am not working?"

I said, "No way. We need it now more than ever. If you are disabled and cannot care for our son, I may have to stay at home more and care for both of you. If that happens, we will need your disability insurance to help provide income to us." As you remember from the start of this chapter, I learned this because of what my mom experienced along with my training to be a CFP® professional. So, of course, we paid the bill.

Fast forward about 3 years later, and my wife started having a problem with her eye. She had lost vision in one of her eyes. She had been going to an optometrist in Walmart for glasses, and she asked him about the issue. He gave her eye drops, but they didn't help. Finally, she decided to see an ophthalmologist. She called me shortly after the scheduled appointment and was very upset. The doctor had examined her eye briefly and said, "You have optic neuritis which is a common side effect of Multiple Sclerosis (MS). You need to see a neurologist as soon as possible." We were floored. Honestly, I did not believe the doctor. I remember saying to Kathy, "What does an eye doctor know about MS?" In fact, I was so sure he was wrong, I almost did not go with Kathy to her neurological consultation the next week. When we saw the neurologist, though, he said that he thought it was MS as well and sent her to get an MRI along with a spinal tap and bloodwork. These tests confirmed the diagnosis, and Kathy has, unfortunately, had to manage this ever since. You see, life's unplanned events on a random Tuesday afternoon are best managed when planned for many years prior to happening.

I say all this to reiterate my point. I didn't know that my wife would need her private disability policy at such a young age, but she did. In fact, she started collecting benefits within several weeks of applying. Meanwhile, Social Security repeatedly turned her down for benefits just like they did for my mom. But, after almost three years of fighting and appealing, Kathy did get approved for Social Security benefits as well. Ultimately, the plan to get the insurance before we needed it allowed us to be in a financial position to fight for the other Social Security disability benefits Kathy paid for through her FICA while she was employed. Unfortunately, my mom could not do this. She worked through the years to the detriment of her health because she did not have this private insurance resource to rely on. My mom had to work through the pain and torment of her disability, which most likely made her disability worse. My wife had a similar situation but a different outcome. The difference was Kathy had private insurance (non-employer based) that paid her right away.

I tell you this journey of mine and the stories that I have been through with clients, along with the science, history, planning, and solutions, in order to help lead you to your own Wealth on Purpose. So, let's look at some tools that you can take and put into action.

Turbocharged Action List #1 (Planning)

- Evaluate your needs and wants.

- Partner with a qualified CFP® professional that has the training or can refer you to needed specialists (attorneys, CPAs, etc.). He/she can help craft this plan and journey.

- If you invest or take action without a plan, that is like taking a prescription without a diagnosis. It is not wise and can be deadly.

- Work with your advisor on the most beneficial Social Security filing strategy for your plan. This should be a household decision. It affects both spouses for life.

- Know that many planning decisions are permanent. How and when to start your pension as well as what to do with your retirement savings plans (401k & etc.) are critical. Get help before you pull the trigger on retirement.

> ## Turbocharged Wealth Rule #1:
> *Plan first, implement after.*

Turbocharged Action List #2 (Risk Management and "Oh, no" Moments)

- You have to play good defense before you play offense.

- Planning should first address risks (insurance needs) and cash reserves. If your advisor does not do this or fails to, you are in the wrong place. If he is scared to talk about these issues, he is not qualified to be your advisor.

- Get proper personally owned life and disability insurance if you have a need. Review and assess the risks and needs of LTC. Evaluate your health and property and casualty insurance needs at least annually.

- Emergency reserves—Have a minimum of 3-6 months of cash reserves (in liquid, safe funds) at all times. If your job is volatile, you may need more. This is not to make money, but to protect you from life's surprises. Placing this where you can gain the best, safe interest while still having access is important as well.

> ## Turbocharged Wealth Rule #2:
> *Prepare for the worst and hope for the best.*

Turbocharged Action List #3 (Buckets)

- Treat your money with purpose. Not all of it will be used at the same time. Treat it that way.

- Just like food, some money is for now (the Grill), some should be for soon (the Fridge), and most should be for later (the Freezer).

- Align strategies and investments with your purpose and buckets of money.

- Don't be afraid of sensible solutions that are new to you.

- Help mitigate bad sequencing of return risk in retirement with this strategy.

- This is a plan that needs to be monitored and adjusted. Don't just "set it and forget it." The great news is that the Bucket Strategy works if times are tough or great, if you have time on your side, or even if you are retired.

- This just makes sense and can work for most people whether you have $1 million or $35 million. Reread Chapter 4.

> ### Turbocharged Wealth Rule #3:
> *Bucket your money on purpose, and it may last you for generations to come. Simplicity on the far side of complexity is genius.*

Turbocharged Action List #4 (Investments)

- You are not going to outsmart the market. The world is littered with great people that tried. Don't pretend you're different.

- You are not going to out time the market. If you try this, you will most likely get it wrong—especially if you have an above-average intelligence level. On the off chance you get it right once, please understand you won the lottery. It was luck, not skill. Reread Chapter 1.

- Sitting on the sidelines "until things get better" is not a strategy. It's market timing and a failed strategy.

- Trying to miss the downsides will almost ensure you will miss the upsides (which happen more often). This is a losing strategy.

- Water cooler talk with your neighbors is probably mostly made up. Truth is, he or she is probably much worse off and has had much less success with his or her investments than you have been told about.

- Use the science of investments to your advantage and structure your portfolio to capture the premiums available in the market. Reread Chapter 5.

- Turn off the financial news media. They are almost always wrong. If it bleeds, it leads. All they want you to do is to watch again tomorrow. They have no interest in your success, nor are they usually qualified to even try.

- A monkey with a dart board can probably outperform your big Wall Street firm's portfolio. If your advisor works for a big proprietary brand, you probably need to leave him. These firms are there to deliver earnings for their shareholders, and that is all. Your big brand advisor is stuck. An independent fiduciary advisor can help remove these challenges from your portfolio.

- Your Bucket 3 (Long-Term) money should be mostly in equities. This is your only hope to combat inflation and taxes. Failure to understand this may cost you and your family for generations. Reread Chapter 4.

- Behavior is what matters most of all in getting a great return. Good investment behavior will beat being "smart" over time.

- Don't let the lizard brain rule you. Reread Chapter 1.

> **Turbocharged Wealth Rule #4:**
> *Proper investment behavior with a purposeful plan using investments that have been structured to capture market premiums is wealth-changing.*

Turbocharged Action List #5 (Taxes)

- This is your biggest lifetime expense. Act like it, and pay attention to it.

- In addition to hiring a good financial planner, partner with a good CPA. They are rare, but they are out there.

- Do tax planning with your advisor. This is NOT tax preparation, so do not confuse the two. They are hardly related.

- The goal should be to lower your lifetime tax payments, not necessarily just this year's payment.

- Withholdings do not equal your tax cost.

- Don't forget in retirement, taxes are still important and may even affect you more.

- Retirees need to know, or be guided by their advisor, about a lot of things regarding taxes, including the control they have over your wealth: RMDs, IRMMA, QCDs, and SS tax. Reread Chapter 6.

- You may be growing a tax problem larger by the year if you have not planned properly. Reread Chapter 6.

- Taxes are complicated and affect your wealth greatly. How you structure your income and investments matters immensely.

> **Turbocharged Wealth Rule #5:**
> *Wealth that is kept is all that matters.*
> *Plan to reduce your tax burden and keep more*
> *of your wealth for generations.*

Turbocharged Action List #6 (Estate, Gifting, and Legacy)

- Estate
  - Control where your money goes or the government will.
  - Get good estate planning documents from a qualified attorney in your state.
  - Review and update these documents as needed, or if your situation changes.
  - Don't just do it the cheapest way.
  - Living trusts can be great, or they can suck. There is not just one answer. Work with your advisor to find a qualified estate attorney.
  - You need documents other than a will (Durable Power of Attorney, Health Care Power of Attorney, and Living Will).
  - Beneficiaries trump your will. Review them periodically.
- Gifting and charity
  - Be generous when you can afford to, not sooner but also not later.

- ○ Be careful in choosing which assets and the method in which to be generous. Not all gifting is created equal.
- ○ Give tax problems (QCD and capital gains) to charity. They are in a 0% bracket.
- ○ Give tax-free or basis-stepped-up assets to family and loved ones.
- ○ Consider a DAF if you own appreciated investments.
- ○ Don't always give your kids cash, consider giving them investments. Reread Chapter 6.
- ○ Consider gifting while you're living to enjoy seeing or experiencing the fruits of that gift in others.

- Legacy
  - ○ If you retire with a successful plan, you most likely won't die dead broke.
  - ○ Have a plan on how, who, when, where, and why someone will get your money.
  - ○ You can change the direction of your family or others with your wealth for generations.

Turbocharged Wealth Rule #6:
Your estate, gifting, and legacy are a part of your wealth.
Make these happen on purpose.

Turbocharged Action List #7 (Implementation, Monitoring, and Advice)

- An unimplemented plan is a dream and serves no purpose. This would have been a waste of time and money. Don't waste your time or money.

- Implement your plan only after having a purposeful plan crafted by a trusted advisor.

- Implementing and monitoring your progress is like wearing the clothes you buy. That's why you bought them. So, make sure to use your plan and monitor it.

- Make adjustments along the way. It is a journey, not a destination.

- Know that wealth is many things. It's not just dollars. It's enjoyment, peace, contentment, and much more. Know that it comes in all shapes and sizes, and one size does not fit all.

- If you think you don't need a financial coach to help maximize your wealth, make sure not to miss a step. By the way, you are probably wrong and will likely cost your family a fortune.

- Don't make the grave mistake of hiring more than one financial advisor. If you have made this mistake, fix it. See Chapter 1.

- Know that financial planning can be fun and meaningful. Done right, this journey to Wealth on Purpose matters. It matters not just to you, but to your family for generations to come. Love them enough to walk this walk.

- Find and hire a trusted financial advisor who will coach you with one goal—Wealth on Purpose.

> **Turbocharged Wealth Rule #7:**
> *Partner with the right financial advisor.*
> *Wealth on Purpose can be in your family*
> *for generations to come.*

This is your recipe to turbocharge your wealth. Now, you just need to go out and make it happen. Find, get, and forever have Wealth on Purpose.

Afterword

Build Your Wealth on Purpose

One of the things I learned very quickly when I entered the world of wealth management and investing is that "Wall Street"—the financial gurus and pundits—are full of promises and claims of overnight riches. The reality is that wealth is built through planning, discipline, patience, and smart investing. Whether it's the promise of big returns from hedge funds or the hype surrounding cryptocurrency investing, there will always be someone promising a quick and easy path to riches.

True wealth is built over time, through a combination of smart investing strategies and the discipline to stay the course, even during market ups and downs. Building wealth is a long and winding road, but it is the prudent and disciplined approach to investing that ultimately wins the day. Building wealth and keeping it is not about listening to the so-called investment news entertainment (financial porn), chasing latest hot investment, or trying to get rich quick. It's about making smart, informed decisions, and having the discipline to stick with your investments over the long term. And that's where we come in!

When I started Ballentine Capital Advisors, my goal was to help clients make smart decisions about financial and investment planning so that they could build a stable and secure financial future for themselves and their families. I wanted to give unbiased, independent, customer-focused financial advice to make sure that my clients didn't have to worry about their money. Since we opened our doors, we have done just that. We now have three financial advisors and a team of about ten. Every day, we strive to give our best to our clients to help them maximize their wealth.

Our core values at Ballentine Capital Advisors are:

- **To provide clients with highly trained professionals to serve their needs.**

- **To always do what is right.**

- **To provide timely, accurate service with a smile on our face and care in our voice and heart.**

- **To do what we say we will do when we say we will do it. We will clearly communicate any problem with the person we are serving, if needed.**

- **To tell our clients what they need to hear, while respectfully understanding this may not always be what they want to hear.**

- **To provide an environment where our team members may lead and achieve a productive and successful professional and personal life.**

- To transparently and eagerly partner with a client to-gether on progress. To communicate both successes and challenges that arise in an open and direct manner with clients in order to achieve success.

- To be good stewards of our community through gener-ously giving of our time and talents which we have been given.

- To treat clients, team members, and our community with care. To strive to add value and happiness to each other and the community we serve.

Why choose us over the bank across the street?

Banks report to shareholders. We report to clients. It is that simple, but the world has made it complex. You should work with an advisor that puts your interest first. If your current advi-sor works for a big brand, his or her first duty is to the bank or brokerage firm he or she works at, not you, the client. That is a bad arrangement for someone to be a trusted advisor.

At Ballentine Capital Advisors, we provide the guidance and personalized attention needed to help you reach your financial goals. Our process involves closely examining each individual to determine your needs and desires, creating a comprehensive financial plan, recommending and executing strategies that are tailored to your unique circumstances, and regularly monitoring and adjusting the plan as necessary. From wealth maximization in retirement to small business planning, we work together to help you achieve the financial success you desire.

Who can benefit from our services?

We are here to help those who have achieved a degree of wealth and are looking to improve their success. For those who have the financial capacity or are likely to have it in the next three years, our services can offer great value. Our wealth management services can help you make the most of your money and create a sound financial strategy that will serve you for years to come.

Our mission is to empower our clients to achieve Wealth on Purpose. We believe that the key to this success is not just in knowledge and understanding of the markets, but also in being equipped to avoid the common behavioral mistakes that can detrimentally impact a portfolio.

We can help protect you from inflation and taxes.

A well-designed wealth plan can be a powerful tool to help you protect your wealth and build a secure financial future. Unfortunately, factors such as inflation and taxes can erode your hard-earned savings, leaving you without the financial security you deserve. To help you stay ahead, it is essential to have a plan to counteract these forces, one that is tailored to your individual needs and goals.

We do not work for Wall Street.

Our commitment to our clients goes beyond providing sound advice. We are dedicated to helping you build a secure financial foundation for your future. We take into account your individual situations and aspirations and strive to provide you with tailored strategies and solutions that will ensure your wealth will provide a lifetime of income and a legacy for future generations. We are not beholden to Wall Street or any other external interests; our only mission is to ensure our clients have the resources to live their lives with financial security and peace of mind.

Investment decisions are important ones.

We are entrusted with some of the most critical decisions a person will make in his/her lifetime, so it is essential that investors structure their portfolio and retirement income in a way that allows them to capitalize on market returns and the market factors that may allow for premiums, rather than relying on stock picking. This positions our clients to maximize wealth and achieve their goals.

You deserve a trusted relationship with a trusted advisor.

We firmly believe you have the right to find the best financial advisor for your needs, and that is a responsibility we would be honored to take on. We understand that we are not the only financial advisors out there and that you may find someone else more suitable for you. However, we are confident that our qualifications and reliability make us a great choice for those who have and want to grow Wealth on Purpose. That is why we strive to be the best in the industry, offering only the highest standard of service and advice. We look forward to the opportunity to serve you and provide you with the peace of mind that comes with trusting in a reliable financial advisor.

As I march through a 25-year career in wealth management, financial planning, and investing, I'm struck by how little has changed when it comes to Wall Street's promises and the gurus and pundits who fill the airwaves and social media. Despite the market's ever-changing nature, they still haven't been able to deliver on the tactics and strategies they hype up.

These days, we have access to more data and information than ever before, but we seem to be starved for wisdom. It's crucial to remember that the best person to look out for your financial future is you, partnered with a trusted advisor who speaks honestly and confidently about wealth and planning.

What has remained true throughout my career is the undeniable fact that economic and global events will always influence investors to make bad decisions and be corrupted by the lizard brain. From market crashes to political unrest, these occurrences can often shake investor confidence and lead them to make decisions that can have long-lasting, negative impacts on their portfolios and wealth. The good news is that we have been able to work alongside many successful families to navigate the challenges ahead and tame the lizard brain.

Still, I remain optimistic and excited for the future. Even though we have seen much global unrest and political bantering that can be nauseating, the future is bright for the next generations. Now more than ever, it is important to take control of your finances and start building a brighter future for yourself and your loved ones. I strongly encourage you to continue to build your Wealth…on Purpose!

Learn more about
Ballentine Capital Advisors

Website: https://ballentinecapital.com/

FB: @ballentinecapital

IG: @ballentinecapital

LinkedIn: @ballentine-capital-advisors

Acknowledgements

To my clients, without you I simply would not be here. Thank you for allowing me to walk beside you in this journey. I am humbled by the opportunity you have given me to help each of you.

To my team at BCA, I am so grateful to you for your contributions to make our clients' lives better and to help them have Wealth on Purpose.

To several long-term team members that have been with me for many years through ups and downs: Katrina Morris, Stephanie Monroe, and Anthony Colancecco.

To my community, I am fortunate to be surrounded by some awesome people in an awesome part of the planet.

To my family and friends that told other potential clients about me, believed in me, and supported me when I was getting this business rolling, especially in the early years.

To my church, Thanks for teaching my family about what is most important, eternal wealth through Christ. Thanks for providing quality education for my children. Thanks for being the best place to refill my tank and providing my family a place to build a foundation on rock.

Ballentine Capital Advisors is a registered investment advisor with the SEC. Information presented here is for educational purposes only and does not intend to make an offer or solicitation for the sale or purchase of any specific securities product, service, or investment strategy.

Investments involve risk and unless otherwise stated, are not guaranteed. Be sure to first consult with a qualified financial advisor, tax professional, or attorney before implementing any strategy or recommendation discussed herein.

Made in the USA
Columbia, SC
03 January 2024

28495124R00080